Morgantown Glass
From Depression Glass
Through the 1960s

Jeffrey B. Snyder

4880 Lower Valley Road, Atglen, PA 19310 USA

To Jim & Marjorie and Jim & Leora.
I could never have done this without you.

Library of Congress Cataloging-in-Publication Data

Snyder, Jeffrey B.
Morgantown glass/Jeffrey B. Snyder.
p. cm.
Includes bibliographical references and index.
ISBN 0-7643-0504-2 (hardcover)
1. Morgantown Glassware Guild--Catalogs. 2. Glassware--West Virginia--
Morgantown--History--20th century--Catalogs. I. Title.
NK5198.M583A4 1998
74k.29154′52--dc21   98-48420
CIP

Designed by "Sue"
Typeset in University Roman Bt and Times New Roman

ISBN: 0-7643-0504-2
Printed in China
1 2 3 4

Published by Schiffer Publishing Ltd.
4880 Lower Valley Road
Atglen, PA 19310
Phone: (610) 593-1777; Fax: (610) 593-2002
E-mail: Schifferbk@aol.com
Please write for a free catalog.
This book may be purchased from the publisher.
Please include $3.95 for shipping.

Please try your bookstore first.

We are interested in hearing from authors
with book ideas on related subjects.

Contents ❄

Acknowledgments ❄

A book like this is always a cooperative effort. I would like to take this opportunity to thank those hard working, knowledgeable, understanding, and patient people who allowed me into their homes for days on end with my formidible tangle of equipment. Special thanks go out to Jim and Marjorie Wiley and Jim and Leora Leasure. Their efforts are greatly appreciated. The beautiful Morgantown glass wares depicted in these pages were provided courtesy of the Leasure and Wiley collections. Jim and Marjorie Wiley also generously provided this author access to their personal research materials.

I would also like to thank the dedicated staff of the West Virginia and Regional History Collection, West Virginia University Libraries. They were able to direct me to many valuable and instructive resources. A special thanks as well to Joseph Gluck and Olive Snyder, both of whom were instrumental in directing me to the West Virginia and Regional History Collection in the first place.

Donna Baker deserves a great deal of credit for all those hours spent capturing the details on that laptop computer.

I also wish to acknowledge Jerry Gallagher, a pioneering scholar in the field of Morgantown glass collecting and the author of *A Handbook of Old Morgantown Glass.*

When searching for antiques or collectibles, there is much to be gained from joining collectors' clubs. For valuable insights, guidance, and general camaraderie, I recommend that Morgantown glass collectors join the Old Morgantown Glass Collectors' Guild, P.O. Box 894, Morgantown, WV 26507-0894.

Finally, I would also like to acknowledge all of the fine, upstanding, and eminently talented individuals who proudly call West Virginia home. Whether I meet you back in our home state or far afield, you are some of the best people that I know.

Introduction ❄

Where workers mingled as a clan
And they were highly paid
And training their apprentices
They kept the tricks of trade.
    The trade was old and started back
    Beyond the Middle Ages
    When windows even one foot square
    Commanded princely wages.
Then in the land of many hills
Was lime and sand and gas
And West Virginia had in plenty
The things to make the glass.

— Oscar DuBois

Just prior to the dawn of the twentieth century, Morgantown, West Virginia, was home to over eighteen thousand individuals. Steam powered locomotives and packet boats delivered people and products regularly to and from this busy industrial town nestled along the banks of the Monongahela River. A combination of natural gas and electricity lit the avenues from downtown to the periphery so well that the local paper proclaimed the city to be the best lit in the state. Local supplies of natural gas also powered Morgantown's diverse and growing industries.

In 1899, Frank Bannister added his contribution to Morgantown's expanding industrial scene, organizing the Morgantown Glass Works. A well known figure in the glassware trade, Bannister had little trouble attracting other Morgantown businessmen to the company.

Between 1899 and 1971, this Morgantown glass factory produced glassware for a wide variety of uses, in thousands of different shapes, styles, and patterns. The company would be best known for the production of handmade, mold blown stemwares and tumblers for both the retail and institutional markets. Included among the institutional markets were American steamship passenger lines, restaurants, hotels, and bars. This prolific factory also produced striking and decorative glassware in the forms of glass baskets, bowls, candleholders, and free-forms, to name a few.

The name of the company would change several times over the years. In 1903, the original Morgantown Glass Works was reorganized as the Economy Tumbler Company. By 1923, this name was considered too restrictive and the corporation became the Economy Glass Company. However, in 1929 the firm's management looked back to the past for inspiration (over the years, company management had referred to their wares as "Old Morgantown" on company logos despite the Economy factory name) and the title Morgantown Glass Works was reinstated.

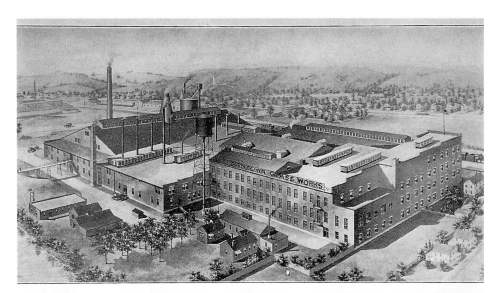

A view of the Morgantown Glass Works factory along the Monongahela River in Morgantown, West Virginia, as it was rendered in the 1931 company catalog.

The Home of "Old Morgantown" Glass, Morgantown, West Virginia

Morgantown Glass Works continued to produce under this name until 1937 when the company, facing financial difficulties, was forced to close. Over the next two years the factory glassware stock was sold off and the company was reestablished as a guild, a cooperative employee owned venture. The factory opened its doors for business again in 1939 with the newly minted name Morgantown Glassware Guild. Although the plant was purchased by the competing glassworks Fostoria in 1965, the factory would continue to produce glassware under the Guild name until it ceased operations in 1971. The plant was then purchased in 1972 by the Bailey Glass Company, but that is beyond the scope of this book.

This text presents a survey of the hand made, mold blown stemware, tumblers, tablewares, and decorative glasswares, their shapes, the decorative motifs applied to these wares over the decades from 1899 to 1971, and the ever changing color palette used to further enhance "Old Morgantown" glasswares. This can only be a survey, as new catalog and advertising copy continues to be found, expanding the range of glass objects which may be indentified as Morgantown glass. A 1929 article in the trade journal *China, Glass and Lamps* succinctly described the range of products produced by Morgantown as, "... an extensive line of stemware and specialties in transparent color as well as in crystal. The factory has quite a large decorating department and many hundreds of pieces are decorated there each day. Etchings, cuttings, and gold, silver, and enamel color work are included in the forms of decorations turned out in the Morgantown factory. Not only has the factory produced all of the more staple pieces of blown stemware and table service, but has introduced many novelties and specialties. It also can and will develop exclusive shapes and patterns for particular services or stores (Chine, Glass and Lamps 1929, 13)."

The history of the firm is presented in three major periods of production familiar to Morgantown collectors as "The Formative Years, 1899-1920, The Years of Elegance, 1921-1937, and The Guild Years, 1939-1971." Catalog pages are included in the discussion of these three periods to aid the reader in identifying the ware types popular in different decades. The majority of the glasswares presented will be found in Chapter 4. All The Wares, organized into categories originally established by the company management and used in their catalogs. Finally, values are also provided with the captions as a guide to what one might expect to pay for the various Morgantown glasswares today.

This Morgantown glass factory produced glassware in many different shapes, styles, and patterns.
A selection of Morgantown cordials: heights range from 3 3/4" to 5 1/2".

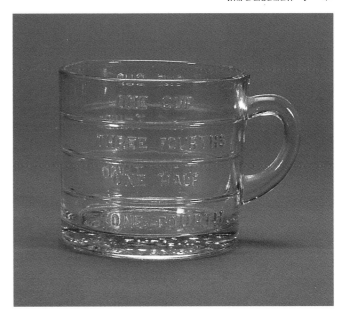

#1021 kitchen cup with molded slogan reading, "Your Credit is Good. Pickering's Complete Home Furnishers, 10th & Penn, Pittsburg" 3 3/4" high x 3 1/4" diameter. Circa early 1900s. $250-300.

#7643 Golf Ball parfait bell in Ritz Blue. Clapper chain is embedded in the glass, indicating that bell was made at the factory, although not necessarily a production item. Circa 1930s. $150-175.

Selection of ivy and witch balls. From left: #64 Coventry in Spanish Red with Crystal foot, 7 1/2" high, $200-225; Ritz Blue with Crystal foot, 6 1/4" high, $225-250; Spanish Red with chimney, 5 1/2" high, $75-85; Stiegel Green without chimney, 4 1/2" high, $65-75.

An assortment of Morgantown shot glasses.

Defining Terms. What's in a name?

Before continuing, it will be useful to identify a few of the basic terms used throughout the book. To begin, while there were many glass factories organizing, manufacturing, and closing in or around the city of Morgantown from approximately the 1890s to the 1970s, when the general term "Morgantown glass" is used here, it is a direct reference to the products of the Morgantown Glass Works factory in one of its various incarnations.

Glass itself is well defined by Robert S. Weiner, in his dissertation *The Location and Distribution of the Glass Industry of Ohio, Pennsylvania, and West Virginia*, as, "...an amorphous substance, usually transparent or translucent, consisting ordinarily of a mixture of silicates, but in some cases of borates, phosphates, etc. Most glass is made by fusing together some form of silica, as sand, an alkali, as pot ash or soda, and some other base, as lime or lead oxide (Weiner 1949, 2)."

The glass produced at Morgantown is generally referred to as **handmade, mold blown glass**. This glassware type was produced by first gathering a small, molten blob of glass on the end of a hollow pipe or rod. Blowing through the pipe and manipulating it in specific ways, a glass worker next preshapes the slowly cooling, glowing mass. The blower then inserts the preshaped "gather" into an iron mold. Blowing into the pipe forces the hot glass to conform to the shape of the inside of the mold. Depending on the specific object being produced, several operations may follow (details of these various operations will be provided in Chapters 2 and 3. Manufacturing Morgantown Glass and Decorating Morgantown Glass). For example, on stemware, the molding of the stem and foot might be done with forms and paddles. Once an item is formed, it is annealed (reheated and allowed to cool gradually and uniformly to avoid shattering the glass) in an oven called a lehr. The cooled object is then sent on for finishing operations, including the removal of excess glass, grinding, and polishing (United States Tariff Commission 1972, A-2).

One glass "decorating" technique directly involved the shape of the interior of the mold itself and is called the "**optic**." The interior of the mold may be shaped in panels, pillars, spirals, swags, and other interesting shapes. These shapes become part of the shape of the body of the glass which is formed in an **optic mold**. The Morgantown glass factory used this technique to good effect, creating a variety of pleasing optics. Many of these optic designs have been named. The "Palm" optic was one of the company's most popular optic designs.

#9932 Carla vase with **Swirl optic** in Steel Blue. 4" high x 4" diameter. Circa 1960s. $25-30.

Assortment of #7673 Lexington with Ritz Blue filament stem and **Palm Optic**. Crystal bowl and foot. Circa 1931.
Back left: 9 oz. goblet. 7 3/4" high x 4" in diameter, $85-95; back right: 5 1/2 oz. saucer champagne. 6 1/2" high x 4" in diameter, $75-85; Front left: 3 1/2 oz. cocktail. 5" high x 3"across, $65-75; front right: 5 1/2 oz. sherbet. 4" high x 4" in diameter, $65-75.

#7711 Callahan champagne and sherbet. #733 Virginia etch. Circa 1920. Crystal. Champagne: 6" high x 4" in diameter. Crystal. Sherbet: 4 1/2" high x 4" in diameter. $18-20 each.

An example of the optic decoration used by the Morgantown plant was discussed in a 1925 article, which stated:

> "Spiral Optic" is the trade name applied to a new design of molded glassware, in the display of the Economy Glass Company, in Room 740 at the Fort Pitt hotel.

#64 Neopolitan 6" diameter ivy/witch ball. 14K Topaz with a **Spiral optic**. Crystal Italian base. Circa 1930s. $700-800.

The spiral and the "Spiral Optic" ware is very distinct, and can be clearly followed from top to bottom. Great care was taken in making the molds to bring out this effect. This design predominates in all table glassware, water sets, vases and novelties (Unattributed article, January 1925).

This mold blown glass process differs from that of companies producing **machine made glass**. In 1972, the Tariff Commission contrasted the two well, stating, "Household glassware similar to types made by Morgantown are also produced by machine. In the machine method, the molten glass is fed in a continuous stream into a forming machine containing the molds; thus machine-made glassware is produced on a volume basis. Machine-made glassware is generally made from **soda-lime glass**, while the handmade glassware produced by Morgantown was made with **low-lead glass** (Morgantown used glass containing 10 to 12 percent lead monoxide) ..." Another term for low-lead glass is "**flint glass**." However, collectors need not concern themselves too much with the visual distinction between soda-lime glass and low-lead (or flint) glass. The commission admitted that most consumers would be unlikely to see much difference between them (United States Tariff Commission 1972, A-1).

In its prime, the Morgantown factory had eighteen furnaces in operation simultaneously. The plant had three furnace stacks. One stack was used exclusively for the production of bar ware. It was separated from the other two because it used soda-lime glass and cheaper materials. The other two stacks were for the company's better glassware lines (Wiley, personal research).

Moving on to specific glassware forms, Morgantown "**stemware**" included goblets, sherbets, tall sherbets or champagnes, cocktails, oyster cocktails, sherries, wine glasses, clarets, and cordial glasses. Included under "**tumblers**" were ice tea, high-ball, old fashioned, juice and water glasses. Morgantown also produced brandy inhalers and "**decorative glasswares**" or "**artwares**" (*see* the Bureau of Industrial Hygiene summary in **Why the Guild Folded, a Summation** at the end of Chapter 1 for the direct reference using the term artware) including baubles, bowls, candleholders, and free-forms—colorful decorative vases and bowls formed without the used of a mold and which have a distinctive flowing shape.

Left: #7711 Callahan 9 oz. Crystal goblet. #733 Virginia etch. Circa 1920. 7 3/4" high x 4" in diameter. $25-28.
Right: #9715 Calhoun 12 oz. Crystal flat-bottom tumbler. #733 Virginia etch. Circa 1920. 5" high x 3" in diameter. $22-25.

Selection of the #7662 Majesty line Spanish Red bowls with Crystal stems and feet. Back row, from left: water goblet, 7" high x 3 1/2" diameter, $70-80; champagne, 6" high x 4" diameter, $60-70; sherbet, 4 1/4" high x 4" diameter, $50-60; ice tea, 5 3/4" high x 3 1/2" diameter, $45-50. Front row, from left: cocktail, 5" high x 3" diameter, $40-45; 5 oz. footed tumbler, 4 1/4" high x 2 3/4" diameter, $30-35; 2 1/2 oz. footed tumbler, 3 1/2" high x 2" diameter, $25-30. All circa 1930s.

#9403—9 oz. tumbler with decoration #507. 3 3/4" high x 2 3/4" diameter. Circa pre-1920s. $50-55.

Selection of #1962 Crinkle line. Back row, from left: LMX 13 oz. footed tumbler in Peacock Blue, $12-15; 6 oz. juice in Gypsy Fire, $8-10; footed tumbler in Evergreen, $12-15; 10 oz. water in Gloria Blue, $8-10. Front row, from left: double old-fashioned in Thistle, $12-15; footed tumbler in Ruby with Crystal foot, $15-22; Tijuana 34 oz. juice/martini pitcher in Lime, $40-50; old-fashioned in Burgundy, $10-12; 6 oz. tumbler in Pineapple, $8-10. Pitcher: 6" high. Glasses range from 3 1/2" high to 5" high. Circa 1960s - early 1970s.

Back: #1800 Free-Form line, in Amberina, 13" long x 8 1/2" wide, $80-90. Front: #1800 Free-Form line in Midnight Blue with Crystal, 12 3/4" high x 4 1/4" diameter, $55-65. Both circa 1960s.

A Word About Collecting, Numbering, Names, and Values

Morgantown glass presents the collector with an interesting challenge. The various stemwares, tumblers, and artwares left the factory with only the packing box (or barrel in the early years) and a paper label on the glasswares to identify them. The vast majority of the boxes and labels are long gone. Also, the unscrupulous have been known to apply bogus labels to glassware and sell it as original "Old Morgantown." Therefore, the collector needs to become quite familiar and comfortable with the various wares produced by the company before seeking out Morgantown glass. It is hoped that this text will provide the collector with a solid foundation of knowledge upon which to build a collection of glassware the collector may be assured is truly Morgantown glass.

Throughout the text, the reader will notice that almost all of the items presented and discussed are preceded by a string of numbers. Old Morgantown glass collectors have continued to use the line numbering system developed by the factory (prior to the firm's acquisition by Fostoria) to identify the glassware lines. A name immediately follows

A larger original Morgantown Glassware Guild, Inc. packing box filled with #113 Sovereign vases. NP.

this number. This is the pattern name. The factory management provided names for some of their pattern lines. However, since Morgantown's management failed to name a number of their pattern lines, collectors have created names for the unnamed pattern lines over the years. All of the established names, whether factory or collector assigned, are presented here for ease of identification and to provide a common ground for discussion.

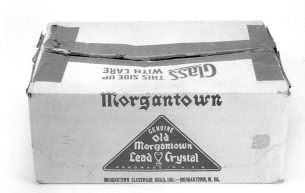

Original Morgantown Glassware Guild, Inc. packing box, complete with a #101 Heritage bowl and two #9935 Barton candleholders. $110-125 including the original box.

Selection of #7690 Monroe line including a goblet, champagne, wine, cocktail, cordial, and three footed tumblers (only one foot per tumbler), Spanish Red bowls with Crystal stems and feet. Back row, from left: 9 oz. goblet, 8 1/4" high x 3 3/4" diameter, $60-70; champagne, 6 1/4" high x 4 1/4" diameter, $45-50; wine, 6" high x 2 1/2" diameter, $45-55; cocktail, 5 1/4" high x 3 1/2" diameter, $30-35; cordial, 4 3/4" high x 1 3/4" diameter, $50-60. Front row, from left: 13 oz. footed tumbler, 7" high x 4" diameter, $35-40; 9 oz. footed tumbler, 6 1/4" high x 3 1/2" diameter, $30-35, 5 oz. footed tumbler, 5" high x 3" diameter, $25-30. All circa 1930s.

The line number and pattern name are followed in the captions with the ware type, color name, and the name of the etching if there is one. The date follows and is given as a circa date in either decade or year. The date indicates when the form is first *known* to be on the market, and this date does not necessarily reflect the first year of production. After the date, the dimensions, and finally the value range are also provided in the captions.

Value ranges for the displayed glassware are provided in each caption. The ranges indicated apply directly to the pieces shown. Establishing a present day value is a delicate thing. Values vary immensely according to the condition of the piece, the location of the market, and the overall quality of the design and manufacture. Condition is always of paramount importance in assigning a value. Prices in the Midwest differ from those in the West or East, and those at specialty antique shows will vary from those at general shows. Of course, being in the right place at the right time can make all the difference.

Furthermore, for glassware produced prior to the Guild years (1939-1971), values vary less, region to region, than for Guild year items. Except in the case of stemwares, color is generally not a major factor in determining the value of pre-Guild glassware.

For stemware produced prior to 1939, Alexandrite is a rare color. Ritz Blue and Spanish Red are the more collectible stemware colors and they tend to carry a higher price than other stemwares of similar age and design. Crystal (clear in color) stemware is almost always found at the lower end of the value scale; however, this does not indicate that a Crystal stem is common, only that it is not considered as desireable as similar pieces in other colors.

Selection of #7643 Golf Ball line. From left: parfait in Spanish Red; cocktail in Ritz Blue; flared oyster cocktail in Ritz Blue; sherry in Ritz Blue. Parfait: $50-60; cocktail: $50-60; oyster cocktail: $50-60; sherry: $35-40.

Left: #7665 Laura 9 oz. goblet. Alexandrite with a Laurel cutting. Circa 1930s. 8 1/4" high, 3 1/2" diameter. $125-150.

Right: #778 Carlton etch. #7606 1/2 Athena 3 1/2 oz. Cocktail. Crystal bowl and foot; Ebony cased filament stem. Circa 1931. 5" high x 3 3/4" in diameter. $65-75.

#808 Mikado etch. #7654 Lorna Ritz Blue 9 oz. footed tumbler, Bohemia painted Gold decoration and #29 border, in Gold. Circa 1930s. 6 1/4" high, 3 .5" in diameter. $80-90.

Values will be higher for desirable stemware patterns on goblets and cordials than for the same pattern in champagnes and sherbets. Common etchings such as Carlton and Mikado are to be found at the lower end of the value ranges ... unless they appear on a particularly desirable stem (e.g. an open or twist stem). As with colors, some etchings are reasonably common but may carry a premium price because that etch is coveted by collectors (such as the Sunrise Medallion and Superba etches).

#758 Sunrise Medallion etch. #9074 Belton 11 oz. footed tumbler. Crystal bowl, Meadow Green foot. Circa 1931. 5 1/4" high x 3 1/2" in diameter. $75-85.

Superba etch. #7654 1/2 Legacy 10 oz. goblet and an Ebony stem. Circa 1931. 8" high x 3 1/2" in diameter. $195-225.

All of these factors make it impossible to create an absolutely accurate values listing; however, a useful general pricing guide may be offered. The values listed here are in U.S. dollars.

As of this writing, glassware from the Guild years (1939-1971) is only now beginning to draw the attentions of collectors. This is especially true of the delicate, beautiful, and colorful wares of Morgantown's Decor Line. Values for this glassware vary widely from region to region. No firm standards have yet been set. Knowledgable collectors are becoming aware of the fact that certain colors are much rarer than others. For example, items in Lime, Peach, and Thistle are much more difficult to find than other colors. Cobalt, Ruby, and White are commonly sought after by collectors and tend to be more costly for it. Nutmeg is a very late color that was produced for a brief period; however, even though it is scarce, it may never be highly valued as it is simply not considered by most collectors to be a handsome color!

I wish you the best of luck in your search for Morgantown glass.

Peach color (opaque). #61 Chanson vase. 8" high x 5" diameter. Circa 1960s. $35-40.

Lime color. #1962 Tijuana 34 oz. crinkle Juice/Martini pitcher. Circa 1958. 6 1/2" high x 4 1/4" in diameter. $65-75.

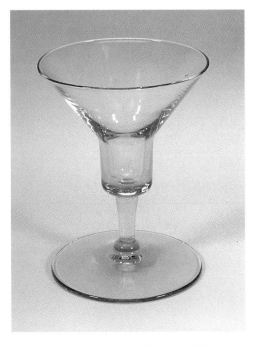

Thistle color. #88 Classic 4 3/4" Candleholder. Circa 1960s. $40-50 pair.

Ruby color with a Crystal handle. #1962 Ockner 50 oz. pitcher. Footed tumbler, Ruby with Crystal foot. Circa 1960s. Pitcher: 8 1/4" high. $115-125. Tumbler: 5" high x 3" in diameter. $18-22.

White color. #3008 White Vision wine with white on white decoration, floral border/band, 6" high. Circa 1970s. Wine: $18-22.

The short-lived and little-appreciated Nutmeg color. Back left: #3019 Pueblo footed tumbler, 6" high x 3 1/4" diameter, $8-10. Back right: #3020 Malta footed tumbler, 5 3/4" high x 3" diameter, $6-8. Front: #3020 Malta wine, 4" high x 2 1/2" diameter, $4-6. All circa 1960s.

Chapter 1. History ❄

Brief histories of the glass industry in America, of changing glass designs, and of the Morgantown Glass Works follow. Being aware of the company history and the changes in glass design over the decades past will help the collector to identify and date Morgantown glassware in the field.

During the nineteenth century, improvements in transportation via canals, railroads, and steamboats opened new glass markets for the glass industry in the United States, particularly in the south and midwest. Glass manufacturers drifted westward, removing themselves from the Eastern Seaboard and establishing factories west of the Allegheny Mountains. The first flint glass works had been established in Pittsburgh between 1808 and 1814. The Zanesville Glass Manufacturing Company of Zanesville, Ohio, followed in 1815. Entering the industry a little later, a flint and cut glass plant was established in Wheeling, West Virginia, in 1831 (Weiner 1949, 20).

With this westward movement came new and more efficient fuels to fire the glass furnaces and increase production. By 1830, coal had almost completely replaced wood. Natural gas was first discovered in Pennsylvania in 1859 and would soon replace coal as the fuel of choice to fire the furnaces. As the years rolled by, additional natural gas wells sprung up in western Pennsylvania, West Virginia, Ohio, and Indiana. As western Pennsylvania's gas wells were depleted, glass plants moved into West Virginia, Ohio, and Indiana to take advantage of fresh gas deposits. In fact, during this period, the developing glass industry followed the newly discovery gas wells like birds following a trail of bread crumbs (Weiner 1949, 20-21).

A large concentration of glass factories developed in West Virginia, Pennsylvania, and Ohio, located roughly between Charleston, Toledo, and Port Allegheny. Within this "glass triangle," the heaviest concentration of factories was located in the northern and western counties of West Virginia and the western counties of Pennsylvania. Out of the factories in this tri-state region would spring all types of glass, from handmade, mold blown tablewares, to mass-produced bottles and free blown art glass. (Weiner 1949, 8; Piña 1995, 6).

The factors determining the location of these glass factories included proximity to raw materials, fuel, and abundant labor, along with access to large markets through reliable transportation systems. Of all these factors, close proximity to a large deposit of high quality glass sand was paramount. Within the "glass triangle," there were two major high grade glass sand deposits. One was located in Berkley Springs, West Virginia, and the other was found in Mapleton, Pennsylvania. These sand deposits are identified as Oriskany Quartzite. They were deposited in this region some 350 million years ago during the Devonian period as a blanket of white marine sandstone seventy-five to one hundred feet thick. The Oriskany deposits provide not only high quality glass sand, but natural gas as well, meeting two of the criteria needed to establish a successful glass factory (Weiner 1949, 25-26; Core 1982, Vol. 1, 31).

Glass factories also needed to be located near their consumer markets. Glass containers and inexpensive pressed or blown glasswares are bulky objects prone to breakage. None of them would support high distribution costs incurred by long distance shipping. The factories of the glass triangle were located in the middle of America's former manufacturing belt (today's "rust" belt), where in 1940 roughly 46 percent of the American population lived and worked (Weiner 1946, 36).

Finally, successful glass factories were located near reliable transportation resources. For the Morgantown Glass Works and other factories of the glass triangle, this transportation source was the railroad. The northeastern quadrant of the United States had the heaviest concentration of railroad networks anywhere within the forty-eight contiguous states. These rail lines provided the glass factories with ready access to their raw materials, to other industrial regions, and to the large urban consumer markets (Weiner 1949, 42).

Nineteenth century technological innovations also accelerated production in the glass plants. By 1850, iron molds were improving glass production, ensuring a greater uniformity among glasswares while reducing the time necessary to create a finished product. Designs carved or cast into the insides of the molds could even imitate the look of expensive hand-cut glass. Glass furnaces were also increasing in size and quality, allowing for higher glass output, a faster working pace, and more routine tasks for workers to perform. As iron molds and improved furnaces became commonplace, glass blowers were no longer required to blow and shape each piece by hand. A number of additional workers now handled the glass both before and after blowing. Among them were gatherers, cracking-off boys, warming-in boys, carrying-in boys, and mold-boys (Zembala 1984, 367). These positions will be further explained in Chapter 2.

As the nineteenth century drew to a close (and the Morgantown Glass Works first opened their doors), the glass industry was rapidly expanding. Consumer demand was on the rise as well. Machinery in the factories was increasing the rate of production and lessening the effects of labor scarcities in some regions. The glass factories themselves were expanding in size and were employing larger numbers of workers than ever before. The glasswares produced by these expanding firms were changing as well, exhibiting new ranges of imaginative shapes, colors, and functions at the dawn of the twentieth century (Weiner 1949, 21-22).

The Evolution of Late Nineteenth and Twentieth Century Glassware Design

In the early decades of the twentieth century, American glass manufacturers were leaving behind the elaborate, expensive, crystal clear nineteenth century Victorian glass patterns just as American potters were shifting from ornate place settings requiring innumerable dishes to simple, streamlined five piece place settings. An article from 1934 stated, "Most factories had kept in mind the great popularity of the buffet supper and created many varieties of articles for the convenience—and pride—of the hostess at such a party (*China, Glass and Lamps* 1934, 11-16)."

Blown and pressed art glass would retain its popularity until around the beginning of the first world war. Brilliant and deeply cut glass, popular near the end of the nineteenth century, was brought back in the early twentieth century; however, by the 1920s this very expensive glassware would fade from the scene as economic depression loomed (Phillips 1981, 206).

Handmade, mold blown glass and machine made glasswares were in direct competition for the consumer's dollars. By the 1930s, roughly half of all the glass produced in the United States would be entirely machine made (Weatherman 1974, 8).

Machine made "Depression glass" (produced from the 1920s onward to the beginning of World War II) glittered on the shelves of the 5 & 10 Cent stores around the country, providing consumers for the first time with useful, inexpensive, complete dinner services and matching serving pieces. Some of the patterns produced were similar in design to the more expensive patterns glass factories were also producing for their wealthier customers (Phillips 1981, 208).

To survive in the competitive marketplace, glass factories had to appeal to a wide range of tastes. Colored glass drew attention in the 1920s and was much in demand in the 1930s. By 1935, roughly half the glass being produced sported colors. Colored glass during the Depression years was generally bright and cheerful. Art Deco colors and shapes were added to glassware lines in the 1930s as well.

The annual Pittsburgh Glass Exhibition was the meeting ground where glass manufacturers displayed their wares to interested buyers and their competition in the trade. The Exhibition was also where future trends were set. An article from 1924 details several of the offerings of the Economy Glass Company, "In Room 740 at Fort Pitt the Economy Glass Company offers a new line of stemware with a green stem and foot, with a most appropriate shamrock design etched on the bowl. Of particularly good shape is the beverage mixer, which is really a cocktail shaker, with a regular shaker top fitted with cork. A funny little pug-nosed sort of lip—if lip can be called pug-nosed—allows beverage to be poured successfully, but is too small to have any effect upon corking or closing of mixer. ... Then, too, there were spiral optic bud vases in tall, slender, fluted shapes in green and crystal and iridescent combinations."

#1 Cadenza 24 oz. cocktail server. #749 Shamrock etch. Circa 1923. Removable top. 10" high. $190-210.

Also detailed in this article were the Economy Glass Company's new offering, Mura Art Glass:

Of Mura Art Glass, a combination of diamond and optic flutes ornament the bowl of these good looking glasses, which have a crystal bowl and foot, the two pieces being joined with an ornamental bit of green glass. There is just enough color in this ware to make it unusually attractive. It is the sort of thing that blends into any decorative scheme for the dining table, for there is just enough green on each piece to successfully supplement the greenery arranged around the flowers. Other colors will be available later. The jeweled stem is made in two parts, we were told, with colored glass worked in as a union between the crystal bowl and foot.

Ten years later, as designs and color variations evolved and diversified, a trade journal article stated that the glasswares presented for 1934 were, "... evolved styles of artistic and commercial importance. Shapes, decorations, color combinations and treatments had all been stepped up to a new 'high' with results that cannot fail to have a profound effect on the trend of the retail market (*China, Glass and Lamps* 1934, 11)."

The 1930s brought about another change that directly affected the glassware industry, the repeal of Prohibition (the 18th Amendment to the Constitution had been ratified January 16, 1919 and went into effect the following year). Edmondson Warrin expounded upon what the end of Prohibition would mean for the glassware industry in his article entitled "And Now—A Toast!" He stated,

With the repeal of the 18th amendment expected in a few weeks, we will come into a period of more dignified drinking. We will watch the bubbles rise in a beautiful champagne glass of fine crystal. Creators of fine things in glass will win a nation back to appreciate the bouquet, color and taste of fine wines.

For this enjoyment we will need finer and more complete sets of glassware, correct glasses for sherry, champagne, Burgundy, white and red wines, Rhine wine and cordials. A woman's set of glassware will mean something to cherish and to show. The hostess in this new era will be deeply interested in what the merchant has to offer for her consideration (Warrin 1933, 13 & 38).

Bar ware and kitchenware were important production items for factories in the 1930s and 1940s, as they could be produced in large quantities at low production costs. Refrigerator storage dishes and ovenproof glass cookware were introduced for the modern kitchen. At times, serving dishes and punch bowls were sold together with metal holders.

Bar wares were important production items for glass factories in the 1930s and 1940s. #28 Waikiki 10 oz. decanter and bar tumbler with Hollywood decoration. Circa 1930s. Decanter: 8" high. $170-190. Tumbler: $35-40.

The 1930s brought about another change that directly affected the glassware industry, the repeal of Prohibition. #2 Victory decanters with octagon stoppers on a tantalis. Crystal with Silver lettering. 8 1/2" high. Circa 1930s. $500-550 set.

After World War II, during the 1940s and 1950s, one of the major design trends developed by American glass designers involved the creation of free blown abstract forms similar to those of European glassmakers. As will be seen later, Steve Britvec, a glass blower since 1948 and foreman of the Morgantown Glassware Guild, produced a number of striking, colorful abstract pieces of fluid design called "free-forms" in the late 1960s. Color, form, and texture all played significant parts in the post-war designs. Many innovative designs were produced in West Virginia. Leslie Piña states, "The hills of West Virginia in the 1950s and 1960s were to American modern glass design what Murano or Orrefors were to European design (Piña 1995, 6)."

#1800 Free-Form line in Amberina, 13" long x 8 1/2" wide. Circa late 1960s. Created by Mr. Steve Britvec of Morgantown. $85-95.

History of Morgantown Glass, the Company and its Wares

"Majestic mountains, picturesque valleys, green rivers and endless mineral resources give to Old Morgantown atmosphere, advantage and environment rich in inspiration for the versatile artists and craftsmen who create the Stemware masterpieces ..."

— Old Morgantown Glass Catalog , 1931

The Formative Years, 1899-1920

In 1899, Morgantown, West Virginia, was a growing town with all the qualities necessary to encourage industrial growth. Morgantown was described in the local paper as follows:

Nature has smiled upon the location of Morgantown in a manner to make her famous for her beauty and health. ... The railroad facilities of Morgantown have added inestimably to her commercial and industrial success ... The Pittsburg, Brownville, Geneva and Morgantown Packet Co. have a line of first-class and elegantly equipped steamboats that arrive and depart daily, affording good passenger and freight transportation. ... Morgantown is one of the best lighted cities in the state. It is brilliantly lighted from center to circumference by natural gas. ... Electricity is also a potent factor as a lighting agent , a great many public and private buildings being lighted by it (Core Vol. IV 1982, 248).

Despite all that light, this kerosene lamp was produced in the 1930s. #64 Lyndale 6" diameter kerosene lamp in Frosted Confetti color with Crystal Italian base. 16 3/4" high. Circa 1930s. $750-850.

In that year, Frank Bannister organized the Morgantown Glass Works along the banks of the Monongahela River. Among the notable local businessmen who joined him in the business were William C. McGrew and Dr. David H. Courtney. William McGrew not only helped to establish the Morgantown Glass Works but also acted as its president for a time. He was also in the mercantile trade, played an active role in the construction of the Fairmont, Morgantown, and Pittsburgh Railroad, was a member of the state senate and house of delegates, and served as Morgantown's mayor (Core Vol. IV 1982, 487). Dr. Courtney was actively involved in setting the course

for the Morgantown firm and was given a great deal of credit for the early success of the company in a trade journal article dating from 1929. His sons were officers in the company and shared his interest in its operation. The early Morgantown Glass Works produced "... a general line of blown tumblers, pressed tableware and pressed tumblers (*China, Glass and Lamps* 1929, 13)."

By 1900, 67 industries operated out of Morgantown. The local population was being affected by the presence of these industries. The 1900 Census found that there were 18,746 native West Virginians in town and 303 foreign-born individuals. This was quite an increase over 1890, when only 74 foreign-born persons were found. The city's new industries, particularly the glass industry, were attracting workers from overseas. The majority of the immigrants were from Germany (97), England (45), Italy (44), Switzerland (33), and France (21) (Core Vol. IV 1982, 253). Over the years, the skills and traditions the immigrating glassworkers brought from their homelands would surely affect the glassware eminating from Morgantown.

In 1903, the Morgantown Glass Works was reorganized and incorporated as the Economy Tumbler Company. The previously produced pressed wares were set aside with the old name and a new line of stemware and bar goods replaced them. The slogan of the company became "Economy Tumblers — Just What The Name Implies!" George W. Fry took the helm as general manager of the glass company briefly from 1903 to 1909. Unlike most of the early supporters of the firm, George Fry was not from

#7810 Monaco 9 oz. Crystal water goblet. #730 Adam etch. Circa 1918. 6" high x 3 1/4" in diameter. $25-28.

Morgantown but was a member of the Fry glass family of Rochester, Pennsylvania. Apparently, all went well in these early years, as in 1905 the *Morgantown Post* reported that the Economy Tumbler Company was expanding the plant. In that year, Morgantown was also noted as the leading glass making city in West Virginia (Core Vol. IV 1982, 314, 322; Weatherman 1974, 280; Gallagher 1989, 8).

Wilbur E. Hunter replaced George Fry as general manager and would remain in charge of plant operations for the next fourteen years, up to 1923. Wilbur Hunter had big plans for the Economy Tumbler Company. On March 27, 1918, the *Morgantown Post* recorded that the Economy Tumbler Company, "one of Morgantown's oldest glass plants," was planning to double its capacity. An article in the trade journal *China, Glass and Lamp* from 1929 would speak highly of the results and of Wilbur Hunter's efforts to improve the factory, "Mr. Hunter rebuilt and improved virtually the entire plant during the period 1917-1919 and the plant today is one of the best equipped and efficiently operated factories in the glassware trade." Hunter's efforts opened the door for the company to begin mass production of colored glassware for both the home market and commercial trade (Core Vol. IV 1982, 476; *China, Glass and Lamp* 1929, 13; Gallagher 1989, 8).

One of the Economy Tumbler Company's catalogs included the following glasswares (and the decorative techniques the company used to adorn them):

Bowls (footed and flat); Bon Bon and Cover; Baskets (Handled); Bitter Bottles; Bar Bottles; Candy Jar and Cover; Candy Box and Cover; Cherry Jar and Cover; Candlesticks; Carafe Sets; Custards (Handled, Handled Cut); Decanters; Finger Bowls; Finger Bowls (Cut); Honey Jar and Cover; Jugs and Pitchers; Marmalade Jar and Cover; Mushroom Covers; Mugs (Handled); Nappies; Nappies (Handled); Oils; Plates; Sandwich Box and Cover; Sugar and Cream; Stemware; Ales; Almond Sets; Cafe Parfait; Champagnes H/S; Cordials; Clarets; Cocktails; Compotes; Egg cups; Grape Fruits and Liner; Goblets - Miscellaneous; Goblets in Lines; Hot Whiskies; Rhine Wines; Sherbets (Footed); Saucer Champagne; Sherries; Wines; Nut Sets; Needle Etched; Plate Etched; Goblets, Cut; Tumblers: *Plain, Handled, Handled and Footed, Band Engraving, Enamel Decoration, Needle Etching, Plate Etching, Bar Cutting, Other Cutting*; Vases; Whiskey Jugs; Water Bottles (Haden n.d., 1).

The Economy Tumbler Company also listed a variety of optics. These included a Spiral Optic, Festoon Optic, vertical line optics—one identified as Optic D.E. 703 (Haden n.d., 16).

Outside of Morgantown, Economy Tumbler Company city sales rooms were located in Boston, Chicago, New York, and Philadelphia. Economy Tumbler glassware was displayed in these cities in the following shops: in Boston

at John J. Reed & Son, 161 Summer Street; in Chicago at Earl W. Newton of 7 North Wabash Avenue; in New York at Cox & Company of 120 Fifth Avenue; and in Philadelphia at Peacock & Roop, 1007 Filbert Street (Haden n.d., 1).

The Years of Elegance, 1921-1937

Company History

Glass production in Morgantown continued to attract glassmakers from overseas. Europeans with glass making talents were frequently attracted by news of the growing American glass industry and crossed the Atlantic seeking better job prospects than those available in the Old World factories. In 1920, 80 Belgian and 35 French immigrants had moved into Monongalia County (within which Morgantown is located), the vast majority of whom arrived to participate in the glass industry in and around Morgantown (Core Vol. IV 1982, 523).

Some of the most beautifully designed and colorful glassware to be produced by the Morgantown factory was created during this period. In 1920, Joseph E. Haden, who would soon prove to be the inspiration behind Morgantown's production of colored glass, was invited to Morgantown by company president Wilbur E. Hunter to be the superintendent of production. He had long experience in the glass industry and had been associated with the Fry Glass Company prior to his move to Morgantown. By 1922, Haden was the factory manager (Gallagher 1989, 8).

Drawing together a team of skilled artisans, Haden and his group developed a wide range of colors and diverse glass designs. In fact, the incorporation of color into the company lines in the early 1920s, coupled with an expanding line of general tableware produced since 1921, would lead the firm to change its name in 1923, shortly after changing company presidents (Gallagher 1989, 8).

In 1923, just prior to the corporate name change, George Dougherty took over the helm as president and general manager from Wilbur E. Hunter. Prior to his association with the Morgantown factory, Dougherty had been associated with the United States Glass Company and the Libbey Glass Company. Dougherty believed the current company name and slogan no longer truly represented the company's products (*China, Glass and Lamps* 1929, 11).

In 1923, the name Economy Tumbler Company was changed to the Economy Glass Company as the production lines expanded to include a more general line of blown tableware, both plain and decorated. The word Tumbler in the company title was no longer adequate to describe the varied and striking wares of the firm. The Economy Glass Company wares were marketed under a triangular label reading "Old Morgantown - Made in USA (*China, Glass and Lamp* 1929, 11; Weatherman 1974, 280)."

Among the new wares were blown, cut and etched wares in many colors and decorative motifs. Blanks (undecorated glasswares) were also sent out by the hundreds for other companies to finish. As production continued to increase, quality rose with it, and critical acclaim soon followed (Weatherman 1974, 280).

In 1926, James Callahan would write the following about the Economy Glass Company and about the glass industry of Morgantown:

> The largest factory is that of the Economy [Glass] Company ... operating mainly under the direction of local capital. The local capital invested in all local glass factories amounts to millions of dollars, and their total annual payroll is about $1,500,000 distributed to nearly 1500 employees ... aside from the University, the glass factories are the biggest drawing card for this city. They furnish employment for many men who have moved to Morgantown to place their children in the State University, and to students who need part-time work to pay their way through the University (Callahan 1926, 269).

In 1929, the management of the Economy Glass Company followed the lead of their own triangular "Old Morgantown" advertising label and once again changed their name. On July 1, 1929, the *New Dominion* newspaper reported that the Economy Glass Company had changed its name to Morgantown Glass Works. The article continues,

> In changing the name back to Morgantown Glass Works, those interested in the progress of the company and its widest possible service in the trade believe that the new name carries with it a more dignified relation to the character and quality of the product and registers the name of the community that views it as one of its leading industrial units.

The triangular Old Morgantown logo used by both the Economy Glass Company and the Morgantown Glass Works that followed. This example appeared in the company's 1931 catalog.

> ... For some time the trade name 'Old Morgantown' has been used by the Economy Glass Company and is rapidly becoming well established in the trade. The linking of the trade mark name "Old Morgantown" with the name of the factory—Morgantown Glass Works— should be an impetus to all connected with the factory (*New Dominion* 1929, 11).

A company advertisement in the trade journal *China, Glass and Lamps*, announced the name change as well. Buyers were asked to remember to, "Use 'Old Morgantown' Glassware for, after all, its—Economy (1929, 17)."

The 1929 *New Dominion* article also lists the officers of the company as George Dougherty, President and General Manager; Joseph H. Courtney, Vice President; Fred C. Lach, Purchasing Agent; David H. Courtney, Jr., Secretary; Joseph Haden, Superintendent; Frank M. Beggs, Service Manager; and Norton C. Boyer, Sales Department. Changes in the firm over the past few years were also reviewed. These included improvements in the general quality and variety of the manufactured line of glassware along with changes in production and distribution which improved the efficiency, service, and quality of the product (*New Dominion* 1929, 11).

Glassware sold from the Morgantown plant was marketed throughout the United States and overseas by 1929. It was reported that "the Morgantown factory has striven to keep abreast of the demand for modern and artistic conceptions in table service and home furnishing"—a far cry from the earlier bar ware products the company had manufactured. The company's longest established sales representative that year was located in Chicago, Illinois. Since 1909, Earl W. Newton Associates had carried products from the Morgantown factory line. By 1929, "Chicagoans" had been raising Morgantown glasses for twenty years (*China, Glass and Lamp* 1929, 11-12).

In 1931, Morgantown Glass Works produced a catalog that has been a boon to collectors. It has provided detailed representations of the wares Morgantown offered that year, allowing collectors to take a close look at the shapes and decorative motifs available in 1931. It also lists all of the colors produced in that year. The catalog states that Morgantown's craftsmen were specialists in delicately blown stemware, of which the factory could boast to more than 500 distinctive stemware patterns for the modern home. Further, these stemware patterns were available "... in nearly a score of colors and combinations of colors ..." The company also took credit for the creation of the "first figured stems, black and colors, encased in crystal." (These cased filament stems will be discussed at length in Chapter 3.) Morgantown Glass Works also introduced the public to its first "open" stems—stems split in a square or diamond shape, leaving a central opening.

Pages from the 1931 Morgantown Glass Works catalog displaying the various wares the company had to offer that year.

Rich Colors
combined with Crystals

The Stemware and miscellaneous Vases and Basket illustrated are produced in several of the warm rich colors for which Old Morgantown is noteworthy. The 7660 Stemware is furnished in Crystal and in Ruby or Ritz Blue combined with Crystal. The 20-4" Basket, 7621-8" Flip Vase, 35½-10" Vase, with handles, and the 35½ Crimped Vase are to be had in Ruby, Ritz Blue, Ebony or the wonderful Stiegel Green with Crystal trimming.

Le Mons

Our 7640 pattern decorated "Le Mons" follows conservatively the art moderne. The angular motif is carried out in the contour of the shape as well as the detail of decoration. The bowls of the Stemware are in Ritz blue with stems and bases on Crystal. The wide Platinum border design illuminates the combination most beautifully. A table setting in "Le Mons" is strikingly handsome. It goes well with warm grays and the dull glow of pewter. Illustrated are the Goblet, Wine, Tall Sherbet, Luncheon Goblet and Salad Plate.

Superba

It is difficult to picture the scintillating beauty of this Formal Dinner Glassware, No. 7664. These tall pieces with their hand-twisted stems cased with Black are unusual examples of the glass working art. The Oriental etching in this two-tone effect is in keeping with the striking shape it embellishes. Your guests will thrill at the luxury of handling these exquisite Tall Goblets, Liqueurs, Cocktails and Tall Sherbets.

Ritz Crystal

A Table Center Service of seven pieces combining Ritz (or Royal) Blue with Crystal. Note the blending of the two effects in the Fruit Bowl, a delicate manipulation of two pieces of glass. A star cut in the bottom increases its brilliance. The identifying numbers are 4355-13" Bowl, 7953 Compotes and 7660 Candles—in deepest, richest Blue that everyone adores. Very definitely in the mode.

Madrid

This group shows four pieces (No. 7665 Goblet, Tall Sherbet, Parfait and Wine) representative of many articles combining the popular Topaz color with Crystal. Topaz, as expressed in this service, is a light color with a tendency toward yellow, but under certain conditions of lighting throws out some of the fiery tints of Amber. It fits nicely into almost any color scheme with neutral calm. The Goblet, Tall Sherbet, Liqueur and Ginger Ale Tumbler bear our catalogue No. 7665 with the decorative etching known as "Madrid."

Majestic

The diamond-like Crystal Glassware of one hundred years ago still survives and, a century from now, Crystal will retain its dignity and be in good taste. The "Majestic" Rock Crystal design is made only in clear, sparkling, twinkling Crystal and will grace the table on which it is used. The 7662 Stemware is our popular chalice shape. Goblet, tall Sherbet, Cocktail, Low Footed Wine and 8" Salad Plate are shown. This ware appeals alike to the most modern and to the most conservative hostesses.

Crystal Black

These covered boxes may be used for candy, to hold a puff and powder, or what you will. They, along with the Compote, are shown here in Crystal glass with a touch of Black now so popular. Any one of them makes a usable gift. The "Witch Ball" Vase has a pastel green globe with Crystal base fashioned in Italian style. It is made also in other colors and combinations. Items shown left to right: 7660 Compote, Black Cased Stem; 2938, 7858 and 9074 covered boxes; 64-6" Witch Ball Vase, Peacock Optic, Italian base.

Fontinelle

A charming pattern that creates a style all its own is "Fontinelle." Combining a duo-tone silvery etching with an artistic touch of Black encased in Crystal stems, it fits admirably with any color scheme. Numbers of items illustrated are listed on page 9.

Informal Glassware

For the informal table these low footed pieces are much in vogue. The departure from the conventional round base to the fancy square design is a smart innovation. The services illustrated at the bottom

Left to right:
7765½—13 oz. Iced Tea
—9 oz. Water Tumbler
—5 oz. Orange Juice
—2½ oz. Wine
—5½ oz. Sherbet or Fruit Salad

More pages from the 1931 Morgantown Glass Works catalog
displaying the various wares the company had to offer that year.

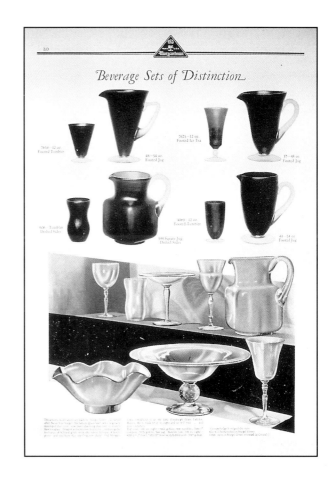

More pages from the 1931 Morgantown Glass Works catalog displaying the various wares the company had to offer that year.

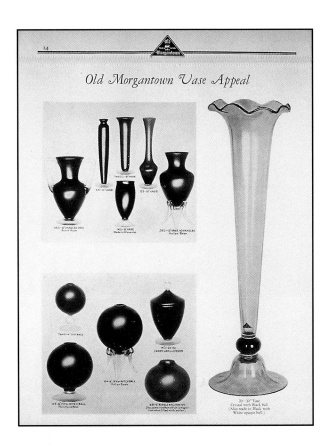

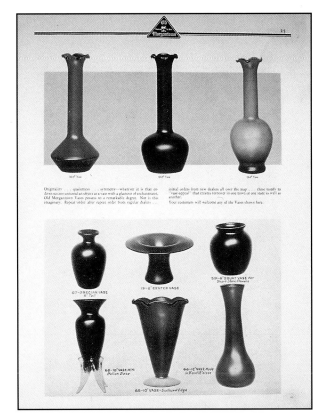

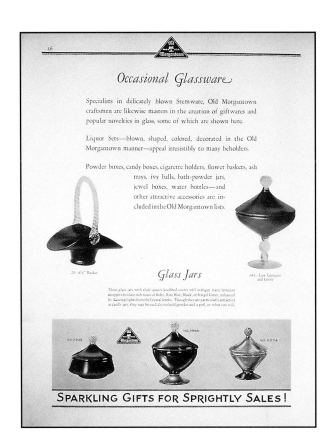

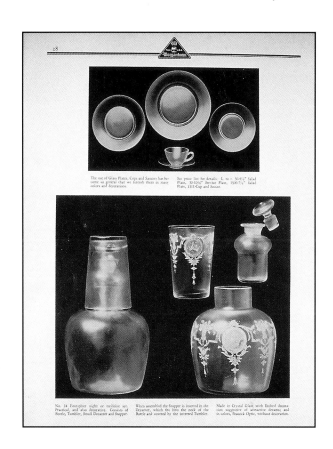

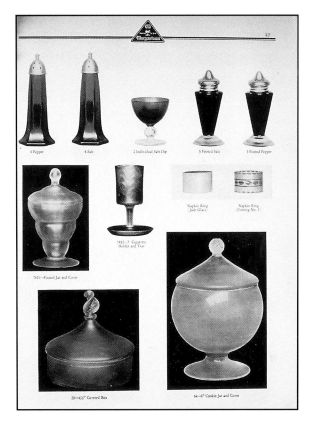

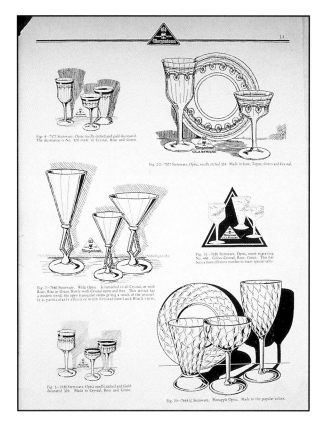

In the 1930s, during the Depression years, Morgantown Glass Works produced large quantities of graceful glassware adorned with elegant decorations and accented with bright, clear colors. Morgantown stemware, plates, and candlesticks added an air of dignity and refinement to the

An effective table setting where the "Fairwin" pattern was used. See Page 17 for close-up illustration.

Attractive display of 7082 Ruby-Crystal stemware. This display "sold out" dealer's stock in 20 days.

This effective table setting, featuring Old Morgantown Ruby-Crystal stemware No. 7082, in Ruby, Crystal, Gold and White was used with marked success by the Nathan Dohrmann Co., of San Francisco. A holly-berry tree in crystal bowl on a handsome mirror plateau was used as the center piece. The glassware was in Ruby and Crystal and the china plates were banded with ruby, encrusted in gold. Broad bands of red satin ribbon ended at each corner with a bunch of red berries, and red tapers were used in the crystal candelabra. This display increased sales—the particular pattern in Ruby-Crystal glassware being sold out completely in a remarkably short time.

Morgantown stemware, plates, and candlesticks added an air of dignity and refinement to the dinner table. The two tables, laden with Morgantown glass, were displayed in the 1931 Morgantown Glass Works catalog.

dinner table. While elegant dinners might be beyond the means of many suffering through the Depression years, striking refreshment, bridge, and luncheon sets would provide a grace note to less expensive functions. Distinctive crystal and colored glassware could be spread throughout the house as well in the form of bar ware, baskets, bowls, candlesticks, candy dishes, and vases. While these items were all quality wares, the vast majority of them were produced at prices accessible to many consumers, even during the Depression years. In truth, these inexpensive, colorful wares—many introduced in 1931—kept the company going during the lean years until the plant closed in 1937 (Gallagher 1989, 11).

Among the colors introduced in 1931 were a "rich, cloudless Spanish Red—at a price as attractive as the stemware," and a color they termed "Stiegel Green," a revival of an early American glass color of the eighteenth century. To add an extra sparkle to the colors, Morgantown Glass Works added a bright Platinum trim to some of their wares.

Note the added sparkle created by the bright Platinum banding. Left: #9719 Circlet tumbler in Ritz Blue with Platinum banding, 5 1/4" high. Right: #9719 Circlet shot glass in Spanish Red with Platinum banding, 2 1/2" high. Circa 1930s. Tumbler: $50-60; shot glass: $65-75.

Selection of #7643 Golf Ball line. From left: ice tea in **Spanish Red**; luncheon goblet in **Ritz Blue**; footed juice tumbler in **Stiegel Green**; wine in **Spanish Red**. Ice tea: $45-50; luncheon goblet: $45-50; juice tumbler: $35-40; wine: $35-40.

The 1931 catalog listed the company's wares and decorations as: Beverage Sets and Items; Bowls; Boxes (Jars); Candlesticks; Color Decorations; Colored Glassware Patterns; Compotes; Cut Patterns; Gold Decorated Patterns; Luncheon Items; Napkin Rings; Needle Etchings; Night Sets; Plates, Cups and Saucers; Plate Etching, Duo Process; Plate Etching, Single Process; Platinum Decorated Patterns; Salts and Peppers; Table Settings; Vases; and White Gold Decorated Patterns.

Bowls were displayed with a variety of edge treatments including crimped, rolled, flared, and scalloped. Compotes were listed as among the best selling of the company's "occasional pieces." These occasional glassware pieces were listed as including Liquor Sets—blown, shaped, colored, decorated in the Old Morgantown manner—; Powder Boxes; Candy Boxes; Cigarette Holders; Flower Baskets; Ash Trays; Ivy Balls; Bath-Powder Jars; Jewel Boxes; Water Bottles; "and other attractive accessories."

The use of glass plates, cups and saucers in 1931 was described by the company as being, "... so general that we furnish them in many colors and decorations." An interesting offering for the night stand was also included as the No. 24 Four-piece night or medicine set. It was comprised of a bottle, tumbler, small decanter, and a stopper. When the night set was assembled, the stopper was inserted into the decanter, which fit into the neck of the bottle, and was covered by the inverted tumbler. It was produced in Crystal glass with etched decoration, in colors, with a Peacock optic, or without decoration. An interesting piece, but this night set seems somehow a bit too complex for someone in need of medicine in the wee hours of the morning.

With the repeal of Prohibition in 1933, a newspaper article in 1934 reported a renewed production demand for glass, china, and pottery manufacturers. "Short stocks in the hands of merchandisers and the change in the status of beer, wine, and liquors brought increased business in china, glassware and pottery at the several January exhibits of 1934 as compared with 1933. New lines, especially in American dinnerware, were received with enthusiasm by buyers (Anonymous 1934, 11)."

This author found two references to workers and working conditions in the Morgantown Glass Works of particular interest during research. The first was in reference to one of the company's long time employees, who had a rather unusual after-hours occupation: "Perhaps best loved of all Morgantown's entertainers was Russel L. Long, who in 1935 was in the midst of a career which extended over a period of more than 60 years." Mr. Long, when not working in the Morgantown plant, was a clown and an Uncle Sam stilt walker in parades. He was born September 27, 1889 in Mount Pleasant, Pennsylvania and came to Morgantown in 1910. Aside from his clowning, Mr. Long was a glass worker employed at the Morgantown Glass Works and he was a member of the Morgantown Flint Glass Workers Union.

The second interesting reference came in the form of an interview with Oscar DuBois, a glassworker who worked in the Morgantown plant on three separate occasions. Mr. DuBois refers to working in another glass plant producing window glass, "They didn't know how to make tanks that would hold out more than 7 or 8 months or 8 or 9 months at most, see. And the tanks would burn out so they had to put the fire out and rebuild the tank. So we always had a long vacation each summer, see, in the window glass. So I happened to be friendly with Mr. Joe Haden. And three different years he gave me some work in there and boy was I like it. I was tickled in there. One reason I liked it so well was, we use to work in the cutting room, we use to work 6 long days at that time. ... And at the—at the flint house in Morgantown, Morgantown Glass they would work five and a half days there so they would quit at noon on Saturday. Boy was I—I had half a day off every Saturday so boy I was tickled about that (DuBois 1965, 22)."

In a March 1935 issue of *Turnover Topics*, a publication available to wholesalers of the day upon request, Morgantown Glass Works stressed the affordability of their Old Morgantown wares. These Depression years were difficult years for most companies. Wide variety, colorful and elegant quality wares, and reasonable prices had taken the company far in the 1920s and early 1930s, but by 1935 the end was near. The next year, Morgantown Glass Works' Board of Directors decided to liquidate their assets, pay off the creditors, and close the plant while they still remained solvent (Gallagher 1989, 11).

Joseph Haden, now vice president and superintendent of the closing firm, remained with the plant in 1937 to sell off the last of the inventory. There was apparently a significant stock, as it took two years to sell the remaining glassware. During this period, Haden developed a plan to reopen the idle plant.

After all, in 1937 West Virginia had 21 plants producing tableware (including pressed and blown dinnerware, stemware, tumblers, bar ware, general table ware, novelties, etched ware, fired ware and cut glassware) to the tune of $13,624,000 annually. West Virginia as a whole contained 22 percent of the entire nation's glass plants and employed over 15 percent of the country's glassworkers. All 58 of the state's glass plants combined were turning out approximately $50,000,000 worth of glass and glassware products of all sorts during that Depression year. So, Joe Haden knew there was money to be made if he could find a way to reopen the Morgantown plant (Bureau of Industrial Hygiene 1937-38, 1-2).

Concept, Color, and Design
Before moving on to see how Joseph Haden reopened the factory idled, a discussion of the elegant glassware colors and designs produced during this period is needed. Joseph Haden was responsible for much of the innovation

in color and design, combined with unique glass treatments, beginning in 1920. During the 1920s and 1930s, this Morgantown glass company would be in the forefront of color, stemware, and etching decoration and design (Gallagher 1990, 39).

#23 Margaret **Jade** guest set with painted (unfired) floral decoration. Circa 1920s. 6" high. $175-195.

This stem displays the Moonstone color. #7654 1/2 Legacy 10 oz. goblet with #758 Sunrise Medallion etch. Circa 1931. 8" high x 3 1/2" in diameter. $175-195.

In January 1923, the Economy Tumbler Company (yet to be renamed), turned heads at the Pittsburgh Glass Exhibition with the introduction of their quality colored glassware, including translucent white, a true green, Moonstone, Jade, Pomona Green, Black, and iridescent treatments (Papert 1972, 280). Of this introduction, a trade journal reported,

> Attractive combinations of colored glass in the form of table and stemware are among the new items being shown in Room 740 at the Fort Pitt by the Economy Tumbler Co., of Morgantown, W. Va. This

company was the first to introduce quality ware in colors and the new offerings are up to the high standard of this factory. In combinations, the white and true green and the moonstone and jade are exceptionally appealing. The white glass is translucent, radiating light instead of absorbing it. Console sets, vases, candy jars, dresser sets, candlesticks, compotes and other articles are in the new color combinations.

During the early-to-mid-1920s, the Economy Glass Company produced several "Two-Tone" covered bowls and boxes. As the company used it, the term Two-Tone was

Two-Tone Danube (Crystal with Nanking Blue trim) small covered box.. Circa 1920s. 4 3/4" high x 4 1/4" in diameter. $175-195.

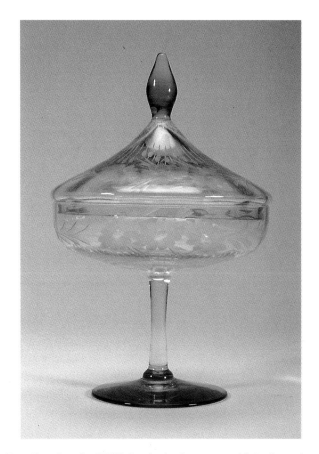

Two-Tone Danube #7801 Cumberland compote with Lydia cutting. 7 1/4" high x 4 1/2" in diameter. Circa 1930s. $250-275.

Two-Tone Genova (14 K Topaz and Nanking blue). #18 Barbara creamer and sugar. Sugar: 6" high, 5" handle to handle; creamer: 6 3/4" high to the lip. Circa 1920s. $275-300 set.

used to identify glasswares manufactured in two colors. The rim of a bowl or the foot and finial of a box would be produced in a different color from the rest of the piece. The remainder of the item was manufactured in a contrasting color. Specific Two-Tone color combinations were given imaginative names by the company. Examples of the known color combinations included for covered wares are Danube (Crystal combined with Nanking Blue trim), Genova (14K Topaz combined with Nanking Blue trim),

Laurel (Crystal combined with Green trim), and Topreen (14K Topaz combined with Pamona Green trim). Five more Two-Tone color combinations were produced, none of which appeared on covered items (*Topics* 1996, 2).

In 1925, the Economy Glass Company would add Amber and Amethyst to their color lines. In 1926, combinations of Yellow and Black, Red and Black, Pink and Magenta, Rose, and a new shade named Rose Amber were all the rage. In 1927, the company introduced a dark Amber. Black combined with crystal was displayed in 1929.

An Amber handle and foot adorn this #37 Barry 48 oz. jug. Crystal Craquelle (crackled) glass, circa 1920s. 8 1/2" high. $325-350.

Amethyst #7662 Majestic 4" low candlesticks with Crystal stems and feet. Circa 1930s. $350-395 pair.

In January 1930, cased filament stemware was introduced, described as a "... black cased stem in combination with crystal bowls and feet, giving the effect of an extremely slender stem in black with all the glitter of crystal. Some of these stems are twisted, and others are straight, but either type is strikingly unusual and charming." Along with the cased stems (and cased swords featuring green or ruby cased colors), a short-lived color named Alexandrite was displayed, described as a new mauve color which was used for a line of stemware called the "Georgian." Alexandrite would not reappear in 1931. Both the Alexandrite color, and an expensive color-printing process were 1930 experiments by the firm aimed at reaching a high-end market. Both apparently failed, as neither were offered again in 1931 (Gallagher 1990, 42).

In 1931, Stiegel Green, Topaz, and Ruby were heralded by the firm. Almost all of the colors introduced would remain on the market for some time, but Ritz Blue, Stiegel Green, Topaz and Ruby would receive the most attention during the 1930s (Papert 1972, 280).

Stiegel Green open compote with a #7688 Jamestown stem. Crystal stem and foot. 4 3/4" high x 6" in diameter. $150-175.

The "... black cased stem in combination with crystal bowls and feet, [give] the effect of an extremely slender stem in black with all the glitter of crystal." #7642 Princess 2 1/2 oz. wine with an Ebony cased filament stem. #777 Baden etch. Circa 1931. 6" high x 2 1/4" in diameter. $95-110.

A 14K Topaz #36 Bolero 54 oz. jug with a Crystal handle and foot and unknown cuttings. 10" high. Circa 1930s. $400-450.

A Ruby #7662 1/2 Jaymar 7 oz. saucer champagne with a Spanish Red cased filament stem. Circa 1930s. $150-175.

To review, the colors listed in the 1931 Morgantown Glass Works catalog include Anna Rose, Azure Blue, Black, 14K Topaz, Jade Green, Meadow Green, Spanish Red, Stiegel Green, Venetian Green, and White Opaque. Jerry Gallagher relates that with the 1931 introduction of Stiegel Green, Morgantown Glass Works had a wider range of intense colors in production than any of their competitors (Morgantown Glass Catalog 1931; Gallagher 1989, 8).

In October of 1931, Morgantown Glass added a new line combining a Ritz Blue glass body with a milk-white trim which they christened "Old Bristol." An advertise-

ment in *The Crockery and Glass Journal* dated December 1932 described Old Bristol as a "...combination of Blue and White ... originated in Bristol, England, at the time George III held sway over the American colonies. It immediately gained royal favor, and shortly thereafter spread to America where it was popularized by the famous glassmaker, Baron von Stiegel. Ritz-Blue glass with milk-white trimming will appeal to your customers, even if they don't know the history. But the Colonial signficance adds tone. And the modern, flawlessly blown shapes by Old Morgantown assure turnover."

In 1933, an article from *The Crockery and Glass Journal* discussed two Morgantown stems noted as technical advances in the art of modern pressed glass. Of the two, the most notable was a split Y shaped stem appropriately named the Yale stem (1933, 10).

The Yale stem. #7684 Yale footed tumbler with a Ritz Blue bowl and Crystal Yale stem and foot. 6 1/4" high, 3 3/4" in diameter. $95-110.

The year 1934 brought a new Burgundy Morgantown color. However, the reporter covering the Pittsburgh Glass Exhibition was much more interested in the wares the new Burgundy color appeared upon — stemware for serving wines and liquors. The stemware bowls were Burgundy and the stems were crystal. Four different decorative styles were shown (*China, Glass and Lamps* 1934, 14).

By 1935, Morgantown's *Turnover Topics* reported that the company's cased stemwares were available in Ritz Blue, Black, Stiegel Green, and Ruby cased filaments— in a variety of shapes (No. 7, 1935).

Old Bristol #6 Kaufmann 54 oz. tankard. Old Bristol combined a Ritz Blue glass body with an Alabaster (milk-white) trim. Circa 1930s. 9.25" high to lip. $1500-1800.

The El Patio line provided the "... perfect glass accessories for vivid peasant potteries ..." Selection of #7696 El Patio line. From left: #7696 El Patio 10 oz. luncheon goblet, Crystal with Stiegel Green foot, 5" high x 2 3/4" diameter; #7696 El Patio sherbet, Crystal with Amber foot, 3 1/2" high x 3 1/4" diameter; same sherbet with Tangerine (opaque) foot; #9075 El Patio cocktail, Crystal with Ritz Blue foot, 3" high x 2 1/2" diameter. Circa 1930s. $25-30 each.

Not to fall behind the times, Morgantown Glass Works also produced El Patio glassware in 1935. These were colorful pieces of informal glassware meant to complement the bright, solid colored, simple ceramic dinnerwares produced by companies such as Homer Laughlin (Fiesta) and Gladding McBean (Franciscan El Patio) which captialized on a growing popular interest in things "South of the Border." El Patio glassware was to be the "... perfect glass accessories for vivid peasant potteries..." The El Patio glass line included footed luncheon goblets, footed juice glasses for breakfast, footed cocktail glasses for parties, sherbets for teas, and Old Fashioneds and Hi Balls for whatever was needed. Colors available in the El Patio line included Amber, Blue, Green, and Tangerine, either solid (but never solid in Tangerine) or combined with Crystal (Haden n.d., 54).

Before turning our attention to the final period of Morgantown glass production, a description of a single glass line featured in the November 24, 1924 issue of *China, Glass and Lamps* will provide an indication of just how extensive a single glassware line during this period could be.

The illustration shows a tall compote of the attractive "Jewel" line, a jelly bowl of medium size and a covered bonbon, the latter two usually requested with the popular apple green stem and foot. According to information given to me by George Dougherty, general manager of the Economy Glass Company and therefore authentic, the line of footed compotes, bowls and fruits is one of the most complete in the industry. Separating these items from the extensive range of Economy products one finds over 100 individual blanks of various shapes and sizes in crystal alone. The crystal number are embellished and decorated with attractive optic designs, colored glass, cuttings, etchings, engravings, etc. to the point where almost any conceivable want may be supplied. They range from the daintiest individual almond to the large 12" fruit bowl and punch bowl in plain blanks or endless forms of decorative treatment.

An example from the Jewel line. #7631 Jewel 9 oz. goblet. Rosamonde etch. Crystal bowl with Meadow Green stem and foot. Circa 1927. 7 1/4" high x 3 1/4" in diameter. $70-80.

The Guild Years, 1939-1971

The *Morgantown Post* reported on January 24, 1939 the reopening of the Morgantown factory as a new entity, "The Morgantown Glassware Guild began operations in the old Morgantown Glass Works, which had been closed since October 15, 1937 (Core Vol. V 1982, 125)." After a hiatus of nearly two years, Joseph Haden saw to the reopening of the Morgantown plant under a new system. Gone were the executive board management and in its place was a guild, a worker owned cooperative factory that would live or die based souly on the efforts of the owner/employees.

The factory property and buildings remained in the hands of the Courtney (remember that Dr. Courtney helped establish the original firm and his sons were officers of the company from its early years) family through the stockholder company, and the Courtneys put up the initial captial to reopen the plant in 1939. However, while the buildings and property of the Guild would remain in the hands of that stockholder company and were rented to the Guild, management of the plant and products were shared by the members of the Guild (Wiley, personal research; Gallagher 1990, 22).

The history of the Guild years breaks down neatly into two periods, the Institutional Years from 1939-1957 and the Decor Years, 1958-1971. The history which follows is broken down into these two very divergent periods of production.

The Institutional Years, 1939-1957

In the first years of production, a number of the more popular lines from the 1930s Morgantown Glass Works continued to be produced. However, the primary focus of the firm between 1939 and 1957 was to produce large volumes of crystal stemware and tableware to be sold almost exclusively to institutional customers. Included among these "institutions" were bars, hotels, railways, restaurants, and steamship lines. This was a lucrative market for the Morgantown Glassware Guild as the company faced little competition from overseas imports. The Guild's major competitors were domestic firms producing entirely machine-made products (Gallagher 1990, 22-23; United States Tariff Commission 1972, 4).

The first few years would be difficult, as the nation was still suffering with the effects of economic depression. World War II would pick up the pace of economic growth for the nation and for the Morgantown Glassware Guild. In fact, in 1941, Morgantown's seven glass factories were all expanding and working overtime to keep up with the demands for bar, table and stemware, illuminating glass products, pressed prism and construction glass products for both the domestic and export markets (Core Vol. V 1982, 141). Of course, during the war, Morgantown did not have to worry about foreign imports competing for the institutional glass customers the firm sought.

Once again, Joseph Haden had Morgantown use color to their advantage. Colored bar and table wares were produced during the 1940s in pastel shades including Amber, Amethyst, Green, Ice Blue, Pink Champagne, and Topaz (Gallagher 1990, 27).

Fiscal success for the Guild brought about stress in the working relationship among Guild members. With heavy sales came the expectation among workers for raises in salaries and benefits. Limiting Guild membership was seen as one way to reduce costs and increase the profits of the current membership. The decision was made to close Guild membership after a time. New hires from that time forward would be company employees and not members of the Guild. The ranks of the Guild's employees grew rapidly during the war years from approximately twenty five individuals to well over three hundred. However, from the day the decision was implemented to close Guild membership, the original Guild concept of employee ownership was altered forever (Gallagher 1990, 23-24).

Throughout the war years, Morgantown introduced new lines and expanded the old, established lines, bringing back some of their production in the retail market trade. Decorative techniques used during the 1920s and 1930s were reintroduced, bringing artisans trained in glass cutting, etching, and decorating back into the Morgantown fold. Etchings dating to the 1940s and 1950s include the #787 1/2 Mayfair, #811 Cathay, #808 Mikado, and "The Drake." Old lines were offered under new names to the

Selection of #6060 Fire and Ice institutional ware. Back row, from left: ale, 7 1/4" high; whiskey sour, 6" high; bowl, 2 1/2" high x 3" diameter; Tom Collins, 5" high. Circa 1940s. Ale: $25-30; whiskey sour, bowl, & Tom Collins: $20-25 each.

retail market in gift shops, department stores, and jewelry shops, all of whom were scrambling for stock during the war years (Gallagher 1990, 24; United States Tariff Commission 1972, 5; Haden n.d., 69).

Competition would be stronger in the retail market than it was in the institutional lines. American manufactured machine-made glassware, domestic handmade glassware (some of which was less expensive than Morgantown's lines), and, in the post-war years, imported handmade glassware would all be challenging the Morgantown Glassware Guild for the retail consumer market (United States Tariff Commission 1972, 5).

In the 1950s, as competition in the glassware market increased, the Morgantown Glassware Guild decided to relinquish control of the plant's production and stock. They returned control of the company to the stockholders company in charge of the physical plant. While the Guild name was retained, all of the workers returned to the status of employees only (United States Tariff Commission 1972, 5; Gallagher 1990, 24-25).

Pages from a 1950s Morgantown Glassware Guild catalog displaying the company's institutional wares for hotels and bars.

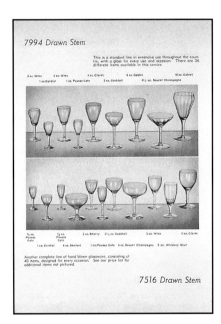

7516 Drawn Stem

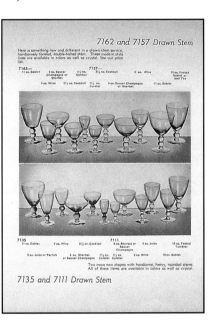

7135 and 7111 Drawn Stem

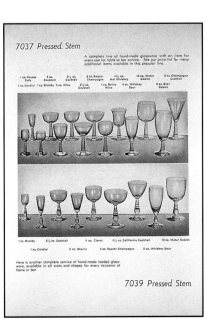

7039 Pressed Stem

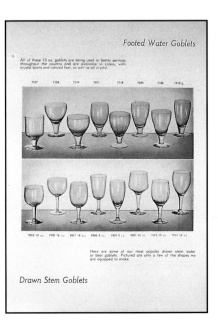

Drawn Stem Goblets

Drawn Stem Cocktails

Pictured are a few of the large variety of cocktails we are equipped to make. Contact the factory for matchings of cocktails not pictured.

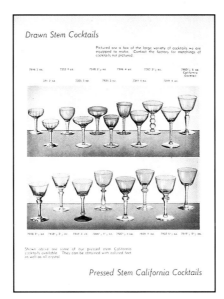

Shown above are some of our pressed stem California cocktails available. They can be obtained with colored feet as well as all crystal.

Pressed Stem California Cocktails

Whiskey Sours; 7163 Drawn Stem

Here are shown a few of the many whiskey sours or parfaits we have available. Also our 7163 group, a short line of drawn stem articles for general bar use.

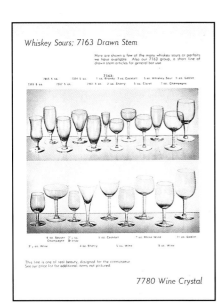

This line is one of real beauty, designed for the connoisseur. See our price list for additional items not pictured.

7780 Wine Crystal

Miscellaneous Items

Here we show a few of the many miscellaneous items available. Contact the factory for information concerning similar items not pictured or shown in the price list.

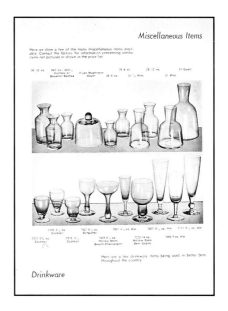

Here are a few drinkware items being used in better bars throughout the country.

Drinkware

9781 1-2 and 9844 Tumblers

Pictured here are two unusual lines that are being well accepted for general bar use. The 9781½ line has a series of four indentations around the base. This makes the tumblers easy to hold as well as adding to their attractiveness. The 9844 line is of an unusual texture, the glass being of a rough, rustic appearance with a heavy square base, swirling into a rounded top. Both these lines are available in colors as well as crystal.

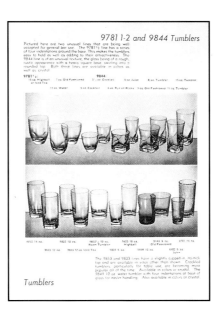

The 9853 and 9833 lines have a slightly cupped-in, no-nick top and are available in sizes other than shown. Crackled tumblers, particularly for table ware, are becoming more popular all of the time. Available in colors or crystal. The 9849 10 oz. water tumbler with four indentations at base of glass for easier handling. Also available in colors or crystal.

Tumblers

7156 and 7158 Low Stemware

Here are two new low lines available in colors as well as crystal.

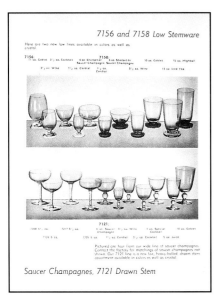

Pictured are four from our wide line of saucer champagnes. Contact the factory for matchings of saucer champagnes not shown. Our 7121 line is a new low, heavy bodied, drawn stem assortment available in colors as well as crystal.

Saucer Champagnes, 7121 Drawn Stem

Cut Flute Tumblers

Here are a few of the many sizes and shapes of fluted tumblers we feature. All popular sizes of whiskeys, old fashioneds, high balls and iced tea glasses are available with different sizes and heights of flutes. See price list for complete schedule.

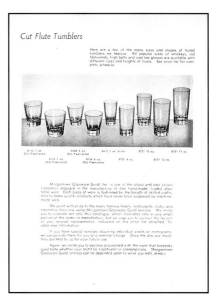

Morgantown Glassware Guild, Inc. is one of the oldest and best known companies engaged in the manufacture of fine hand made, leaded glass table ware. Each piece of ware is fashioned by the breath of skilled craftsmen to make quality products which have never been surpassed by machine-made ware.

We point with pride to the many famous hotels, restaurants, clubs, and steamship lines now using Morgantown Glassware Guild services. We invite you to examine not only this catalogue, which illustrates only a very small portion of the items we manufacture, but we urge you to contact the factory or your nearest representative, indicated on the price list attached, for additional information.

If you have special services requiring individual crests or monograms, we can provide them for you at a nominal charge. Once the dies are made, they are held by us for your future use.

Again we invite you to become acquainted with the ware that bespeaks good taste whether your motif be traditional or contemporary. Morgantown Glassware Guild services can be depended upon to serve you well, always.

Whiskey Glasses

Pictured are various sizes and shapes of whiskey glasses. We have available many more not pictured in capacities from 1½ oz. to 3½ oz.

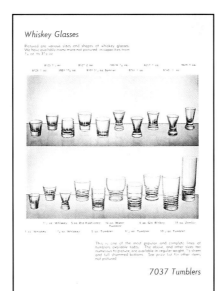

This is one of the most popular and complete lines of tumblers available today. The above, and other sizes too numerous to picture, are available in regular weight, ½ sham and full shammed bottoms. See price list for other items, not pictured.

7037 Tumblers

In 1952, Joseph Haden retired from the Guild, leaving the management of the plant to his sons, Samuel K. Haden (president and general manager) and J. Richard Haden (vice president and superintendent). Taking the helm, the Haden brothers quickly produced a company catalog for their sales representatives featuring numerous glasswares pulled from established lines with good track records, many of which could be directed toward institutional and commercial clients. The majority of wares presented were available in Crystal. Available colors were largely relegated to contrasting colors on the stems and feet (Gallagher 1990, 26-27).

Specific and distinctive molds were manufactured during this period to produce stemware design specifically for private clubs and clients. These are now highly-sought by collectors. Among these stemware designs are the Jockey Stem, the Mai Tai Polynesian Stem, and the Top Hat. Also produced at this time were an Owl tumbler and the Chanticleer Cocktail stemware. The Chanticleer has a rooster-shaped stem joining the bowl and foot. The Chan-

Three Top Hat cocktails, made for the Knickerbocker Hotel. From left: Spanish Red bowls with frosted stem and Crystal foot, $125-150; Crystal bowl with Amber stem and foot, $125-150; Ritz Blue bowl with Crystal stem and foot, $95-110. All 5" high x 3" diameter. Circa 1940s.

Examples of the 1950s colors (not always relegated to stems and feet) are shown in this Harlequin set of #644 Corday 1 1/2 oz. handled cordials (#221 made for Marks and Rosenfeld). Colors, working left to right, back to front: Topaz Mist, Amethyst, Smoke, Coral, Smoke, Shamrock Green, Copen Blue, Gloria Blue. 3 1/2" high, 2 1/2" diameter. Circa 1950s. $20-30 each.

Chanticleer cocktail. Ruby bowl with Crystal foot and stem. Circa 1950s/1960s. 4" high x 3" in diameter. $50-55.

Guild provided a much more extensive listing of the institutional buyers of their wares as well. In the 1950s, these included:

Hotel Taft, New York; Hotel St. George, New York; Carlton House, New York; Hotel Savoy Plaza, New York; Hotel Sherry Netherland, New York; Hotel New Yorker, New York; Hotel Astor, New York; Virgin Isle Hotel, Virgin Islands; Desert Inn, Las Vegas; Chambord Restaurant,

ticleer cocktails were sold in sets of eight in a rainbow assortment of colors, at $3.00 a set. Each Chanticleer cocktail was decorated in a different color within the set. The available pastel colors included Amber, Amethyst, Azure, Light Blue, Blue, Champagne, Coral, Green, Rose, and Smoke. Chanticleer cocktails were also produced in all Crystal and in Ruby and Crystal as well as Ritz Blue and Crystal combinations. Another stemware line highly prized from this period is the Summer Cornucopia line, in which the delicate stems are molded in the shapes of horns of plenty, each horn filled to overflowing with glass flowers (Gallagher 1990, 26-27; Haden n.d., 70-72).

In 1952, the *Morgantown Post* reported that the Guild produced 3600 dozen sets of glassware for the luxury liner *United States* (Core Vol. V 1982, 260). The Morgantown Glassware

Institutional ware wine and brandy with the El Morocco hotel etch. Crystal with Ritz Blue foot. Circa 1930s (this was obviously a durable line of institutional ware produced by Morgantown for many years). Wine: 5" high x 2 1/4" in diameter. $40-45. Brandy: 4" high x 1 1/2" in diameter. $45-50.

A selection from the delicate #8446 Summer Cornucopia line. Circa 1950s. Back left: 7 oz. saucer champagne. 5 1/2" high x 4" in diameter. $150-165. Back right: 1 oz. cordial. 4" high. $225-250. Front: 4 oz. cocktail. 5" high x 3" in diameter. $125-150.

The initials of the Illinois Railroad adorn this #7011 institutional ware Hartley goblet. Crystal bowl with a Ruby foot. Circa 1940s. 5 3/4" high x 2 1/2" in diameter. $35-40.

New York; Brussels Restaurant, New York; Hotel St. Regis, New York; Hotel Ritz Carlton, Boston; Hotel Carlyle, New York; Colony Restaurant, New York; Versailles Restaurant, New York; Biltmore Hotel, New York; Park Lane Hotel, New York; Commodore Hotel, New York; Jack & Charlies "21" Club, New York; El Morocco, New York; Stork Club, New York; United States S.S. Lines, New York; American Export S.S. Lines, New York; Ambassador Hotel, New York; Leone's Restaurant, New York; Sardi's, New York; Carlton House, Pittsburgh; Schenley Hotel, Pittsburgh; Matson Navigation Co., San Francisco; Isthmiann S.S. Co., San Francisco; Edgewater Beach Hotel, Chicago; Hotel Drake, Chicago; Hotel Cleveland, Cleveland; Frisco Railroad, Chicago; Illinois Central R.R., Chicago; Hotel Webster Hall, Pittsburgh.

The Guild also provided deep etch crests and initials for their institutional customers upon request. It is not uncommon to find the crest or initials of railway and steamship lines on Old Morgantown bar ware from the 1950s.

Beginning on April 1, 1957, five Morgantown glass companies joined in the summer festivities celebrating the 350th anniversary of the founding of Jamestown, Virginia. Included among the Morgantown glass firms were the Morgantown Glassware Guild, the Beaumont Company, Davis-Lynch Glass Company, Seneca Glass Company, and Quality Glass Company. Keep an eye out for special

Morgantown glass provided for this celebration (Core Vol. V 1982, 316).

By the late 1950s, the Guild's business with the institutional market was slipping. Well-known restaurants and night clubs were closing their doors and American steamship service was diminishing. Many hotels that had made use of handmade, mold blown glassware were switching to less expensive machine-made glassware to reduce costs as motels and moter inns cut into hotel profits. Accordingly, the Haden brothers would turn Guild production away from institutional wares and toward the retail market (United States Tariff Commission 1972, 4-5).

The Decor Years, 1958-1971

In a company produced pamphlet, *The Fire That Never Dies*, the Morgantown Glassware Guild stated that their production during this period was aimed at and included the following,

> Most of the hand-blown table glassware made by Morgantown goes into the home, owned and prized by people all over the world. Stemware and goblets and vases and pitchers and candle holders and all sorts of other fine glassware come from our factory. Actually, we have molds and equipment to produce some 5,000 different items! (n.d. 13-14)

Samuel and J. Richard Haden would produce high quality lead glass in both traditional and modern designs during this period. The Old Morgantown label would boast that their products were "Genuine Lead Crystal, Handmade in the USA." As with all of Morgantown's most successful lines, the late 1950s and 1960s glassware would once

The late 1950s and 1960s glassware would once again emphasize color. The "My Daddy Dressed Me" ensemble of Morgantown colors. Back row, from left: #9902 Flamenco vase in matte Moss Green, 12" high, $25-30; #1160 Baronet urn in Bristol Blue, 6 3/4" high, $30-35; #65 Withers 6" compote in matte Gypsy Fire, $45-50. Front: #9937 Revere 4 1/2" bowl in Amethyst, $30-35. All circa 1960s. Note: "My Daddy Dressed Me" is *not* a Morgantown company pattern name.

again emphasize color. The greatest success of the period would be the introduction of Richard Haden's new Decor Line in 1958. The Decor Line featured glasswares in modern shapes and brilliant colors which Leslie Piña describes as "... consistent with contemporary trends for bold and innovative design in all the decorative arts." New colors would be developed for the line regularly which, combined with elegant angular shapes, would further distinguish the Decor Line (Piña 1995, 114).

The New Decor Line was introduced in a color catalog produced by the Haden brothers in 1958 and aimed at interior decorators who were looking for colorful glassware in new shapes every year to complement their interior design. J. Richard Haden had designed most of the Decor shapes and colors himself. Decor colors introduced over the years from 1958 to 1970 are included in the table that follows (Gallagher 1991, 46).

Decor Color	Year First Issued
Burgundy	1958
Crystal	1958
Evergreen	1958
Lime	1958
Peacock Blue	1958
Pineapple	1958
Ruby	1958
Steel	1958
Bristol Blue	1961
Peach	1961
Gypsy Fire	1962
Thistle	1962
Moss Green	1964
Ebony	1966
Nutmeg	1968
Gold	1969
Midnight Blue	1969
Cobalt	1970

These early 1960s Morgantown Glassware Guild catalog pages (pp. 1-4) show the various glassware products of the Decor Line.

This is a Morgantown Glassware Guild catalog from the early 1960s. The catalog includes J. Richard Haden's Decor Line and the President's House Line, among other items.

More early 1960s Morgantown Glassware Guild catalog pages (pp. 5-7 and 11) show the various glassware products of the Decor Line.

The 1960s President's House line from the early 1960s Guild catalog.

Martini sets, tumblers, "drinkware," and beverage sets shown in the early 1960s Guild catalog.

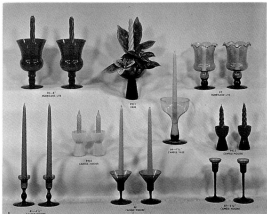

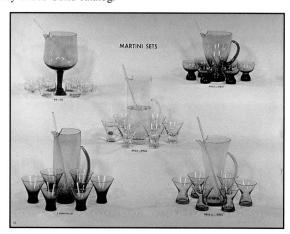

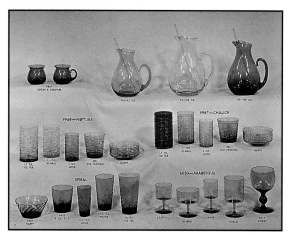

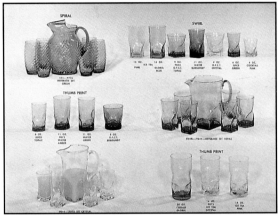

On January 11, 1959, former president and general manager of Morgantown Glass Works George Dougherty died. He was described in the obituary as a pioneer in Morgantown's handblown glass industry and the president of the First National Bank (Core Vol. V. 1982, 336).

In 1963, the Morgantown Glassware Guild advertised a leaded crystal glassware line called "The President's House." First Lady Jacqueline Kennedy had personally

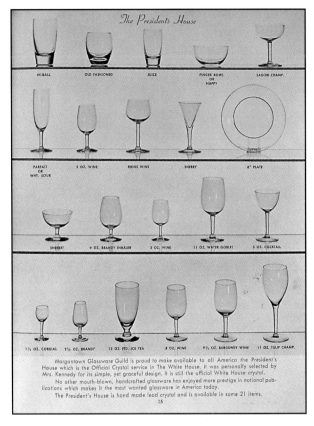

A table set with early 1960s glassware produced by the Morgantown Glassware Guild.

Above and right: #7780 President's House juice. Decorated with Seal of the President of the United States. 4" high. Circa 1960s. $35-40.

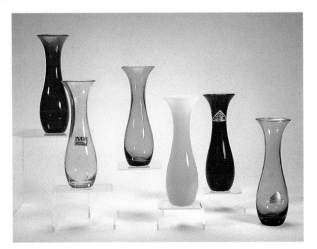

A sampling of the 1960s Decor line colors used by the Morgantown Glassware Guild. #9933 Grace vases displayed in the following colors (left to right, back to front rows): back row: Gypsy Fire, Peacock Blue, Ruby; front row: Pineapple, Bristol Blue, & Moss Green. 6" high, 2" in diameter. Circa 1960s. $10-12 each.

chosen this glassware line as the "Official Crystal Service" of the White House. It was a very simple, straight-forward glassware design. President's House glassware was identified with a paper label that read "The President's House/ Handmade Lead Crystal/by/Morgantown." Shown in an early advertisement were three items from the line including an eight inch plate, an Old Fashioned tumbler, and a Rhine Wine goblet. In 1967, The President's House line would return to the news as the glassware pattern chosen by Lynda Bird Johnson for her December wedding (*The Fire That Never Dies* 12; Core Vol. V. 1982, 431).

In 1963, Joseph Haden, the long time leader of the Morgantown glassware industry and color glass innovator, passed away on October third. Born in Monaca, Pennsylvania, on June 7, 1884, Joseph Haden had moved to Morgantown in 1920 to head the Economy Tumbler Company and had remained with the firm to produce memorable glassware right on through to the Morgantown Glassware Guild period. He was survived by his wife Stella (Kramer) Haden, his four sons Samuel K., J. Richard, Charles H., and Robert P. and two daughters, listed only as Mrs. J.C. Gingrich and Mrs. John Reynard (Core Vol. V. 1982, 385).

Signed "Sam and Dick Haden," the final Morgantown Glassware Guild catalog produced while the company was under Courtney family ownership was printed in 1964. The company logo read "Genuine Old Morgantown Lead Crystal. Handmade in U.S.A." and the glass colors available that year were Steel Blue, Peacock Blue, Burgundy, Golden Moss, Gypsy Fire, Ruby, Crystal, Amber, Pink, Gloria Blue, and Topaz. A matte finish was also available for colored glassware.

By the mid-1960s, company stockholders were aging and looking for a way out of the business. While employment at the factory was up, the physical plant and melting equipment were old and in need of repair. The Courtneys accepted an offer from the Fostoria Glass Company of Moundsville, West Virginia, to buy the Morgantown Glassware Guild, Inc., on March 1, 1965. The announcement was made jointly by Samuel Haden and Robert F. Hannum, presidents of the two merging companies. A letter to that effect was sent to company customers on April 2, 1965 (Gallagher 1991, 47).

Fostoria allowed the Guild to operate unaffected for one year, giving Fostoria a chance to observe and integrate Morgantown's production strategy with their own. After that time, the Haden's influence on design and color diminished and Richard Haden's Decor Line was phased out, replaced by lines developed by the Fostoria design department in Moundsville.

A 1970 Morgantown Glassware Guild catalog displaying the wares produced by the company under Fostoria ownership. The President's House line remained, but many of the designs displayed were developed by the Fostoria design department in Moundsville, West Virginia.

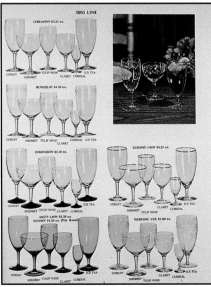

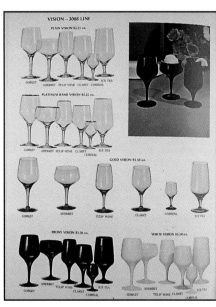

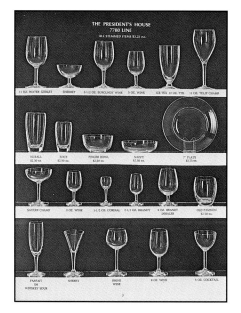

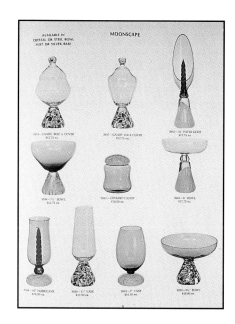

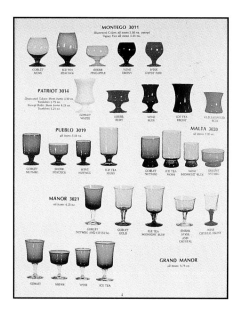

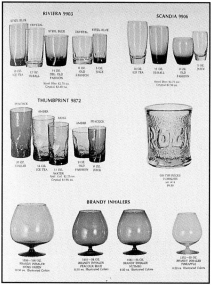

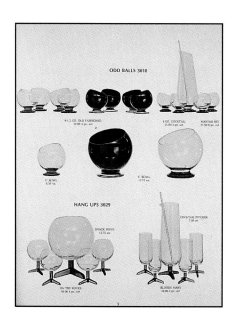

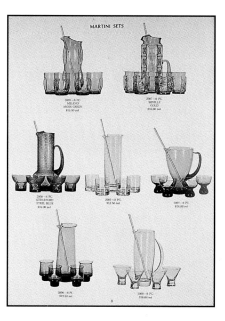

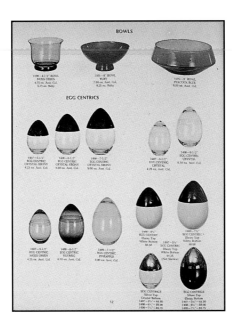

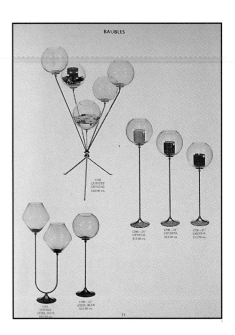

More of the 1970 Morgantown Glassware Guild catalog.

Stemware lines produced during the Fostoria years from 1965 to 1971 included these patterns: Ceremony, Dimension, Ebony Vision, Grand Manor, Gold Vision, Leading Lady, Malta Pattern, Manor Pattern, Misty Lady, Montego, Patriot, Platinum Band Vision, President's House, Pueblo, Riviera, Rondelay, Scandia, Sonnet, Thumbprint, Vision, Wedding Veil, White Vision.

Under the heading "Miscellaneous Items," were Baubles, Bowls, Boxes, Brandy Inhalers, Candlelites, Cocktail Sets, Egg Centrics, Flowerlites, Hang-One-On, Hang Ups, Martini Sets, Moonscape Gifts, Odd Balls, Stack Jar, Stemware, Super Wines, Tumblers, Urns, and Vases.

The colors produced during the Fostoria ownership of the Morgantown Glassware Guild included Amber, Cobalt, Crystal, Ebony, Gold, Gypsy Fire, Midnight Blue, Moss Green, Nutmeg, Pineapple, Peacock Blue, Ruby, Steel Blue, and White (Haden n.d., 101).

On October 8, 1969, the *Dominion-News* reported that Samuel K. Haden had resigned and had been succeeded by Thomas G. Lightner as president of the Morgantown Glassware Guild (Core Vol. V. 1982, 468). By 1970, Guild catalog sales were declining. In April of 1971, the Morgantown Glassware Guild, Inc., was closed by Fostoria. Several days after the 200 remaining employees were let go, Richard Haden oversaw the final closing of the plant and the extinguishing of the furnace fires (Gallagher 1991, 51).

A selection from #1962 Crinkle line. Back row, from left: LMX 13 oz. footed tumbler in Peacock Blue, $12-15; 6 oz. juice in Gypsy Fire, $8-10; footed tumbler in Evergreen, $12-15; 10 oz. water in Gloria Blue, $8-10. Front row, from left: double old-fashioned in Thistle, $12-15; footed tumbler in Ruby with Crystal foot, $15-22; Tijuana 34 oz. juice/martini pitcher in Lime, $40-50; old-fashioned in Burgundy, $10-12; 6 oz. tumbler in Pineapple, $8-10. Pitcher: 6" high. Glasses range from 3 1/2" high to 5" high. Circa 1960s - early 1970s.

When the Morgantown Glass Company went out of business in 1971, the Seneca Glass Company finished the Carboné contract. The close-up shot of Pineapple tumbler shows the Seneca sticker. The sticker reads "By Seneca, Patent No. 170666, Hand Blown." $8-10.

Why the Guild Folded, a Summation

The United States Tariff Commission investigated the complaints of Morgantown Glassware Guild workers who were seeking compensation for the loss of their jobs, blaming unfair foreign competition for the closure of the Morgantown plant. The findings of the Commission were surprising and provide an interesting look at the last five years of the firm's history.

The Commission divided the Guild's business into three categories, the institutional market, the artware market, and the retail market. In the institutional market, the Commission found that Morgantown faced little or no competition from foreign imports. "The company's loss of sales in that area resulted from declining demand for handmade glassware and the encroachment of domestic machine-made ware. ... a survey ... of several of the largest institutional glassware customers of the firm revealed that, with the closing of the Morgantown plant, these customers all switched to other domestic manufacturers of either machine-made or handmade glassware, rather than to importers, as a source for their requirements of glassware (1972, 4)."

With the loss of institutional sales, Morgantown Glassware Guild attempted to increase sales in the retail market, in part, by expanding production of glass artware. The Commission concluded that this move was unsuccessful. The Guild experienced strong competition, predominantly from domestic glass artware and domestic artware manufacturers of wood, plastic, and other non-glass artware materials (United States Tariff Commission 1972, 4-5).

Finally, in the retail market, competition with the Guild in their last five years stemmed from three sources: domestically produced machine-made glassware, domestically produced handmade glassware, and imported handmade glassware. The most serious competition facing the Guild in this arena was from machine-made glassware, which accounted for the vast majority of the glassware sold domestically (92%) between 1965 and 1970 (United States Tariff Commission 1972, 5, 7).

A *Morgantown Post* article from April 1971 had declared that the Morgantown glass companies were all in danger of closing, unable to face the threat posed by foreign glass (Core Vol. V 1982, 487). The Guild workers cited foreign glass as the reason for their plant's closure. Sadly, the Commission found that the Guild's failure stemmed from threats much closer to home. In the end, a course was set for the Morgantown Glassware Guild that guaranteed they would be unable to compete with their domestic rivals. The best selling, imaginative wares of the Decor Line were stripped from the catalogs. Nothing that could compete with the less expensive, domestically produced, machine-made glass was manufactured in the final five years of the firm's production.

Morgantown Glassware Guild employee service awards, made into a necklace and ring. The workers blamed foreign competition for the closure of the Morgantown Glassware Guild factory; however, the real problems that finally closed the plant were much closer to home. NP.

Chapter 2. Manufacturing Morgantown Glass

Manufacturing Morgantown Glass

The basic information about how Morgantown produced its glass was provided by a company printed pamphlet entitled *The Fire That Never Dies*. This brief discussion provides a working overview of how glass was manufactured at the plant and presents useful terminology associated with the manufacture of glass. To begin with, the basic materials needed to produce glass include very fine silicate sand, soda, and lime ... along with varying quantities of added material such as potash, nitre, and lead to control the quality. Added together in carefully measured amounts in a large wooden box, the resulting mixture is called the "batch." A typical batch for table ware includes sand, potash, lime, borax, sodium diuranate, sodium tartrate, and saltpeter (Bureau of Industrial Hygiene 1937-38, 11). As a finishing touch, scraps of broken glass, called "cullet," are added to the top of the batch.

The pamphlet *The Fire That Never Dies*.

This paperweight is filled with colored glass cullet. NP.

Piece of Gypsy Fire cullet made into a ladies ring. NP.

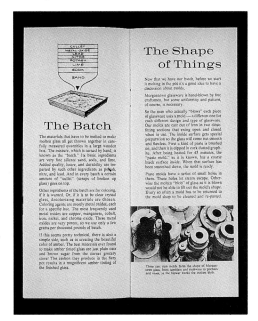

A diagram of the batch and an illustration showing the molds used by Morgantown from *The Fire That Never Dies*.

Extra ingredients may be added to the batch to produce varying glass colors. Decoloring materials might also be chosen if a batch of crystal clear glass is to be made. Coloring agents consist primarily of metal oxides. The most commonly used metal oxides include chrome, copper, cobalt, iron nickle, and manganese. Coloring agents are powerful, only a few grams of metal oxides are required to color a thousand pounds of batch.

The furnace temperature necessary to work molten glass at Morgantown ranged between 2,400 degrees and 2,600 degrees Fahrenheit. Twenty-eight hours in the fire were needed to transform a batch into molten glass. In the molten state, glass is referred to as "metal."

In the early 1960s, when this pamphlet was written, the Morgantown Glassware Guild factory had an eighteen pot furnace, the only one that was still in existence at that time. The pots themselves were made of a clay composite that was gradually seasoned and preheated to 2,000 degrees before being placed into the furnace, where new pots remain for twenty-four hours. At that point, cullet was added to the pot. Once melted, the cullet glazed and coated the inner surface of the pot to reduce corrosion. Only after this process was complete, was a new pot ready to produce molten glass.

As it took twenty-eight hours for batch to heat into molten glass, half of the eighteen pots in the furnace were fed a load of batch at the end of each day. The other nine pots were filled with molten glass, which was then planed off (impurities were removed from the surface) to clear glass "metal" ready for work. This rotation kept every other pot ready for work on any given business day. Each pot would produce approximately one ton of metal, enough molten glass to turn out between 1800 and 2500 pieces of handmade, mold blown glassware. At the time this pamphlet was written, the Morgantown factory was producing between 16,000 and 20,000 glassware items every day.

From the molten "metal," Morgantown produced hand-blown glass shaped in molds. A different iron mold was manufactured for each and every glassware design and type. The molds were cast iron, made in two close-fitting sections that swung open and closed when in use.

Before the molten glass could be blown into the mold, the mold's inner surface had to be prepared. To ensure that the glass would come out smooth and unmarred, a paste was applied to the inside of the mold. Then the paste mold, as it was referred to, was dipped in cork dusted graphite. The mold was then heated for forty-five minutes, creating a coarse black surface inside. When this surface was smoothed down, the mold was ready for the glass.

Paste molds of this sort have a series of small holes in them designed to allow steam to escape, displaced by the expanding mass of the molten glass as it fills out the mold's interior shape. After repeated use, a mold had to be taken back to the mold shop to be cleaned and pasted again.

A group of glass craftsmen working together at a pot was called a shop. Two shops generally worked every pot of prepared "metal." The average shop producing straightforward pieces such as tumblers and stemware included four individuals. They were the gatherer, the blower, the cracking-off boy and the carrying-in boy (or girl). Do not let the names fool you, the average "boy" or "girl" in a shop was a full-grown adult member of the American Flint Glass Workers Union.

First the gatherer would take a long, hollow metal rod and thrust its bell-shaped end into the pot of metal. Molten glass would gather at the bell-shaped end to the rod. Once the proper amount of glass was gathered to the hollow rod, the gatherer would remove the rod from the pot, place the white hot glass blob on a "marver," a highly polished piece of steel, and turn the rod to pack and shape the glass. Once the glass at the end of the rod was prepared, the gatherer would blow a short burst of air into the hollow rod and hand it over to the blower.

Then the blower would spin the rod until the sidewalls of the molten glass were even. Standing on a platform above an iron mold (the opening and closing of which he controlled with foot pedals), the blower placed the hot glass

Two Morgantown glass molds, shown with two Morgantown factory oven bricks and glass blower's tools (hollow rod and cutting shears). NP.

Into The Pot

Above and right: Various gathering, blowing, and shaping techniques displayed in the company pamphlet, *The Fire That Never Dies.*

Manufacturing Morgantown Glass 53 ❈

Prior to the journey through the lehr, the glassware was cooling down much too quickly. Unless the rate of cooling could be slowed and made uniform thoroughout each piece of glassware, the unevenly cooling surfaces would shatter. To avoid this messy and expensive disaster, every blown glass item made a slow two hour journey on a metal mesh conveyor belt through the lehr. Within the first third of the lehr, fire boxes maintained a high but gradually cooling temperature beginning at 900 degrees Fahrenheit. Passing through the lehr, the glass was slowly cooling and toughening in a process called "annealing."

Glassware rolling out of the far end of the lehr was cool to the touch. At this point, a first selection for imperfections was made. Pieces with obvious flaws were set aside and broken to be used as cullet in a future batch.

From the lehr, the glass was taken to another room filled with cutting and finishing machinery. Once there, the glass cap was removed. The cap was that part of the glass attached to the end of the blower's rod while the glass was formed in the mold. To remove the cap, a carborundum stone set at a predetermined height made a slight horizontal scoring mark on the glass. Then the glass was placed in a turning chuck (a device that held the glass in place) and inserted into a circular burner with a hot, piercing flame. The excess top immediately cracked off at the score mark. Now the rim of the glass had to be smoothed to remove sharp or jagged edges left behind when the cap cracked-off.

The glass was given a water rinse and sent on to a rapidly moving carborundum stone or belt which smoothed down the roughness at the rim. At this point, the rim was straight but it was also extremely sharp. Once the glass had air dried, it was sent on to a glazing machine that took the glass through a series of very hot flames. The glass rotated rim-up under the glazing flames and the sharp edge would melt just enough to roll smoothly while gaining a sparkling fire-polished finish.

Now the glass was again inspected. Glass not requiring decorating was then packed for shipment. In the end, a plain mold blown drinking glass required the skills of fifteen people to complete.

Pressed Glass Components

While much of the Morgantown glassware produced was blown into the mold, pressed glassware was part of the total package since the company's founding. Well known Morgantown stemware components were produced using pressed glass manufacturing techniques. These include some of the more elaborate stems, such as stems that feature open square or diamond shapes within the stem and the cased filament stems to be discussed in detail later. These pressed stems were attached to mold blown bowls. To produce pressed glass, a hot glass gather was placed in the mold and then pressed into all parts of the mold by a

into the open mold and then closes the mold around it by stepping on the foot pedal. Blowing into the hollow pipe, the blower expanded the hot glass evenly into a progressively thinner glass shell that approached the inner walls of the mold. The blower kept turning the rod in circles while blowing until he felt the glass was tight enough in the mold to be well formed.

Depressing the foot pedal again opened the mold and the formed piece of glass was removed. The formed pieced had a cap at the end where the rod extended down into the mold. This glass cap would later be removed.

The blower handed the rod and formed glass piece over to the cracking-off boy who carried it over to an asbestos-covered "cradle." (Of course that was back in the 1960s and one hopes that the cradles in current use are no longer asbestos-covered!) Using a chisel-shaped tool, this worker "cracked" the blown glass item away from the rod's end and into the cradle. At this point, the glass had cooled somewhat and was hardened enough to hold its shape; however, cool is a relative term as the glass was still over 1000 degrees Fahrenheit.

From the opposite end of the chisel-like tool, the cracking-off boy employed a two-pronged fork to safely lift the glass item. He placed the object in front of a current of cool air wafting from a nearby pipe. The rapidly cooling glass was then placed upon a metal plate.

Within minutes, the carrying-off boy came by with a multi-pronged rod and lifted the several glass items that had accumulated on the metal plate away from the furnace area. He carried them to a conveyor belt which took the glassware on a slow trip through the lehr—the oven designed to slowly and uniformly cool the glass.

plunger. This process was in common use in glass factories from 1827 onward (Papert 1972, 6).

An article dated January 1926 discussed a new pressed glass line first displayed in Room 740 of the Fort Pitt Hotel earlier that month by the Economy Glass Company. While unnamed by the reporter, the line was described as, "The initial pressed line is made in larger table pieces and has flutes around the bottom of the pieces or the base of the bowls. This is shown in colors applied in the factory's own decorating shop. These colors are in combinations of yellow and black, red and black, and pink and magenta."

A fine example of the cased filament stem. #7701 Fischer parfait. Crystal bowl and foot with Spanish Red cased filament stem. 6 3/4" high x 2 3/4" diameter. Circa 1940s. $65-75.

Here are wonderful examples of various pressed stems. Back row from left: #7636 Square flared bowl 9oz. goblet with #763 Maryland etch. Crystal bowl with Anna Rose stem and foot, 8" high x 4" diameter, $175-200; #7637 Courtney cupped bowl champagne in Crystal with satin stem, 6 1/2" high x 4 1/4" high, $160-185; #7624 Paragon 10 oz. goblet with Crystal stem and foot, 8" high x 3 3/4" diameter, $125-150. Front row, from left: #7637 Courtney wine in Crystal with satin stem, 7 1/4" high x 2 3/4" diameter, $160-185; #7623 Pygon icer (minus liner), Crystal bowl with satin stem, 5" high x 3 1/2" diameter, $125-150; #7623 Pygon wine, Crystal bowl and foot with satin stem and rose cutting, 5 1/2" high x 2 1/4" diameter, $150-175; #7623 Pygon ice tea, Crystal bowl and foot with satin stem and wheat cutting, 7 1/2" high x 2 3/4" diameter, $125-150.

Chapter 3. Decorating Morgantown Glass

There were many ways to decorate Morgantown glass. They range from surface decorations and surface shaping in the form of Optics on to internal decoration in the form of cased filament stems and controlled bubbles within the stems. Decorative techniques employed by the firm, and by other glass manufacturers, will be discussed here beginning with surface decoration (decorations either applied onto or into the surface of glass blanks) and working our way in to the internal cased filaments and controlled bubbles. Specific examples will be shown to illustrate the techniques used by Morgantown.

Surface Decorating Techniques

Applied Rims

The applied rim was a decorating technique in which a band of glass with a contrasting color was bonded to the edge of a piece of glassware. Some of Morgantown's most striking glasswares have applied rims. Such wares were never produced in large numbers and are now considered to be scarce.

Forming applied rims is a decorative technique originating in Europe. It is most likely that one of the immigrant artisans brought the technique with him to Morgantown (Wiley 1997, 2-3). Examples of Mogantown glassware with applied rims include the following lines:

Old Bristol bowls, compotes, and jugs: the Old Bristol line was produced in the 1930s and combined Ritz Blue glassware with an Alabaster trim or vice versa.

A Ritz Blue applied rim provides a bright contrast to the Alabaster body of this Brittania line bowl. 13" in diameter. $800-900.

Old Bristol line #6 Kaufmann 54 oz. tankard. Ritz Blue with an Alabaster applied rim and handle. Circa 1930s. 9.25" high to lip. $1500-1800.

Left and below: Two-Tone Genova #25 Phillipi 12" diameter bowl. Circa 1920s. $350-400.

Two-Tone bowls: Two-Tone was an artware line produced by Morgantown in the early 1920s and several color combinations are known to exist (Wiley 1997, 2-3).

Individual pieces of Morgantown production glassware featuring the applied rim include:
#4355 Janice bowls, both with plain and rolled rims;
#4355 Janice bowl with a crimped rim;
#4356 Irene basket;
#4356 Irene console bowl (Wiley 1997, 2-3).

#4355 Janice 13" Spanish Red console bowl with a rolled rim and applied Crystal edge. Circa 1930s. 13" in diameter. $375-425.

#4356 Irene 10 1/2" bowl-shaped basket in Stiegel Green with an applied Crystal rim. Crystal twisted reed handle. Circa 1920s. 11" high x 10 1/2" in diameter at the widest point. $825-875.

#37 Barry jug, Meadow Green cased Alabaster with non-cased Meadow Green foot. #7637 Bartley footed tumbler with Meadow Green cased Alabaster with non-cased Meadow Green foot. Circa 1930s. Jug: 8.5" high to lip. $500-550. Tumbler: 6" high, 4" in diameter. $125-140.

Cased Glass

Cased glass shows two different glass colors together. The inside of the cased glass is generally white and the exterior is some other, bolder color. Large cased glass items include Morgantown pitchers and vases. To created cased glass, the gatherer first gathers a blob of white on the end of the hollow blow pipe, blocks it with a small wooden block, and blows the white blob into a small ball. Once the white ball of glass has cooled enough, another color (such as Spanish Red for example) is gathered over the top of the white ball. The blocker then blocks the two-colored mass round in a metal or wooden block and hands the blow pipe off to the blower. The blower carefully blows the hot glass into shape prior to blowing it into the mold. There are various operations which could be performed on the hot glassware once it is removed from the mold. For example, the handle would be attached to a pitcher and the spout would be formed by shearing (Britvec 1992, 2).

At this point, it was critical that both glass colors have similar expansion and contraction properties as they cool together in the lehr. If the colors were incompatible, they would cool at different rates. This would lead to the glass separating, cracking, or shattering (Britvec 1992, 2). In the next section, moving to interior decoration, Morgantown's cased filament stems will be discussed.

Color Banding, Lining, and Painting

As these are similar processes, they are combined here. These processes should not be confused with metallic band decorations applied with an electroplating process.

Color banding materials were very finely ground and thoroughly dry. They were usually mixed, a small amount at a time, with fat oil of turpentine or oil of copaiba. Decorators then applied the color to glassware with a fine brush. The use of a decorating wheel greatly accelerated the application of horizontal lines (Bureau of Industrial Hygiene 1937-38, 41-42).

Machines were developed to apply simpler types of linings. For machine use, the color was mixed with water and alcohol or water and glycerine. It was applied to rotating glassware with tracking wheels or discs (Bureau of Industrial Hygiene 1937-38, 41-42).

Painted designs were often produced by first printing the outline of the design onto the glass with a steel plate transfer process (discussed below) and then filling in the open spaces of the design by hand, using a variety of colors (Bureau of Industrial Hygiene 1937-38, 41-42).

Cutting

Prior to glass cutting, selectors inspected finished blown wares. Once defective items were removed, the remaining wares were sent on to the markers. Markers used either red lead and oil of turpentine or stencil ink to mark the general outlines of the pattern on the glass for the cutters. Lines and dots were used to indicate exactly where the cutters were to place the designs (Bureau of Industrial Hygiene 1937-38, 37-38).

Marked wares were sent on to miter cutters, flute cutters, or stopperers. The flute cutters cut flutes into the bases of glasses by holding a glass against a horizontal wheel made of either sandstone or aloxite. Aloxite was a crystalline alumina abrasive containing small impurities (Bureau of Industrial Hygiene 1937-38, 37-38).

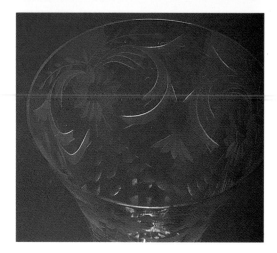

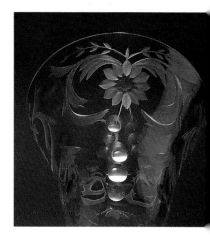

Above and right: Flirtation cutting on a #7642 Princess 9 oz, goblet. Crystal with Venetian Green stem and foot. Flirtation cutting. 8 1/2" high x 3 3/4" in diameter. $70-80.

Butterfly and leaf cutting on a #8 Orleans 54 oz. jug. Crystal. Circa 1920. 8" high x 4 1/2" in diameter. $150-175.

Above and right: Floral cutting on a #7813 Chapman 2 1/2 oz. wine, Crystal with Nanking Blue foot. Circa 1922. 4 1/2 " high x 2" in diameter. $25-28.

Eton cutting on a #7643 Golf Ball 12 oz. ice tea in Crystal. Circa 1930s. 7" high x 3 1/4" in diameter. $40-45.

Floral cutting on the foot of this #7643 Jacobi 4" Crystal candleholder. Circa 1931. 4" high x 3" in diameter. $250-275 pair.

Floral cutting (of the fronds below the etched flowers—to clarify: this etch and cut combination was identified as the #727 Victoria Regina) on a #7640 Art Moderne 9 oz. goblet. #727 Victoria Regina etch combined with a floral cutting of the stems and leaves. Circa 1931. Crystal bowl and foot. India black stem. Circa 1931. 7 1/2" high x 3" in diameter. $125-140.

Lydia cutting on a #19 Kelsha 12" bowl. Two-Tone Danube. Circa 1921. 7 1/2" high x 12 1/2" high. $350-375.

Grape cutting on a #19 Kelsha 12" bowl. Two-Tone Danube. Circa 1921. 8" high x 12 1/2" in diameter. $350-375.

Pandora cutting on a #16 Rachel 5" covered bon bon. Crystal. Circa 1920s. $225-250.

#507 Iroquois cutting on this #8711 tumbler, 5 1/2 oz. Circa 1920s. Tumbler: 3 3/4" high x 2 1/2" in diameter. $25-30.

Laurel cutting on the #7665 Laura 9 oz. goblet. Alexandrite color. Circa 1930s. 8 1/4" high, 3 1/2" diameter. $125-150.

Rock Crystal cutting on this #7691 Monica 10 oz. goblet. Crystal. Cut stem and foot. 8 1/2" high x 3 1/2" in diameter. $50-60.

Look carefully on the far right and you will find a Rose and Wheat cutting. The Rose cutting appears on a #7623 Pygon wine. This wine glass has a Crystal bowl and foot with satin stem. It measures 5 1/2" high x 2 1/4" diameter, and is valued at $150-175. The Wheat cutting appears on the #7623 Pygon ice tea on the far right. This ice tea has a Crystal bowl and foot with satin stem. It measures 7 1/2" high x 2 3/4" diameter. $125-150.

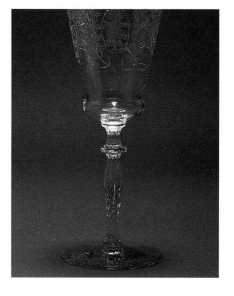

An example of a cut stem. #7691 Monica 10 oz. goblet. Crystal with Rock Crystal cutting. Cut stem and foot. 8 1/2" high x 3 1/2" in diameter. $50-60.

Shasta cutting on a #25 Olympic 12" vase. Crystal. Circa 1920. 12" high. $125-135.

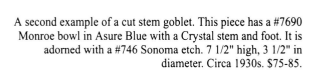

A second example of a cut stem goblet. This piece has a #7690 Monroe bowl in Asure Blue with a Crystal stem and foot. It is adorned with a #746 Sonoma etch. 7 1/2" high, 3 1/2" in diameter. Circa 1930s. $75-85.

Miter cutters produced a variety of designs using high speed aloxite wheels with edges dressed to create desired types of cuts. Water was continuously dripping on the wheel during the cutting operation to increase the speed of the cutting.

Stopperers, or stopper grinders, placed a stopper in a lathe. While holding the bottle, the stopperer grinds the stopper into the bottle with the help of emery dust. At times the stopper and bottle neck were left rough, called "frosted," following the emery grinding. Otherwise, they were polished with fine sand, producing a clear and transparent neck and stopper (Bureau of Industrial Hygiene 1937-38, 37-38).

An example of the "frosted" stopper. The stopper and bottle neck have been left rough following the emery grinding on this #2124 Regina Spanish Red decanter with its Crystal octagon stopper with applied Platinum decoration. Circa 1930s. 10" high. $350-390.

After the cutting was complete, the glass was either polished by a hand polisher or it was given an acid polish. To acid polish a piece, it was dipped into a hydrofluoric and sulphuric acid solution until the rough cuts were polished. Pure hydrofluoric acid was not used as it would not produce a good final polish. The acid polisher wore rubber gloves, apron and boots, and handled racks of glassware, being careful never to allow his hands to come in contact with the acid solution. The acid vats were hooded and exhaust fans removed the fumes. Following the acid bath polishing, the glassware was carefully washed and polished with a cloth (Bureau of Industrial Hygiene 1937-38, 37-38).

Hand polishing was accomplished with a cork wheel coated with pumice paste. The polisher used this wheel to polish each cut on every item. This was a labor-intensive job requiring more time than the actual cutting had originally taken. Smears or dark spots could be created around the cuts using this process if the glass was pressed against the wheel too hard and became heated. These imperfections would require subsequent removal by a buffer using a hard pressed felt wheel and putty. The putty was made from a special mixture of lead and very fine pumice (Bureau of Industrial Hygiene 1937-38, 37-38).

On hollow wares, a rough spot was left on the base of the glass where the ware had been stuck to the punty rod. This spot was ground off by a punty grinder or punty bottom boy using a steel wheel and powdered emery. The emery was kept wet during the punty grinding (Bureau of Industrial Hygiene 1937-38, 37-38).

Once the hand polished ware was finished, it was washed in soap suds and polished with a cloth (Bureau of Industrial Hygiene 1937-38, 37-38).

Decalcomania Transfer

This type of transfer decoration was useful for both glass and pottery (as were other forms of transfer printing). The transfer color was very thin, full of varnish, and difficult to fire glossy at glass decorating temperatures. Opal glass gave the best results with this decorative technique (Bureau of Industrial Hygiene 1937-38, 44-45).

In this transfer method, a grease composition impression of the lines and areas of a single color of the design are made on a fine grained limestone. The stone is treated with diluted nitric acid for a short period. The acid attacks the uncovered portions, leaving the greased areas slightly raised. In printing, a water dampened roller was run over the stone, followed by a roller wet with varnish. Decalcomania paper was then printed with varnish. The color was then dusted onto the paper and rubbed into the varnish. After the first color had dried, other colors were printed on the same sheet from other prepared stones. Once complete, the entire design was given a varnish coat to prevent the color from dusting off and to assist in transferring the design to the ware. Most decalcomania paper is duplex paper composed of very thin tissue mounted on a heavy backing paper (Bureau of Industrial Hygiene 1937-38, 44-45).

To make the transfer, the glassware was first coated with a thin layer of varnish. The tissue with the design was then removed from the heavy backing paper and placed onto the varnished glassware with the design side next to the glass. The tissue was then smoothed down and rubbed with a stiff brush to ensure that the design was in complete contact with the varnished glass. The paper was then soaked off in lukewarm water, leaving the finished design behind on the glass (Bureau of Industrial Hygiene 1937-38, 44-45).

Etching

Both the needle and plate etching were acid etching techniques. Glass companies all assigned specific numbers to each of their etchings for identification. Glassware companies also frequently contracted out to other firms to provide etched decorations for the company's glass blanks. While it is well known that etching was done within the walls of the Morgantown glass factory, there is little documentary evidence to suggest exactly how much of the etched decoration appearing on Morgantown glass was done in-house and how much was contracted out to other firms (Wiley 1996, 3).

Needle Etching

This processs requires both a complex and intricate machine and a skilled setter who must be able to adjust the machine to create the proper pattern. The first step in the needle etching process was to dip the ware to be etched in wax. The "dipper" performs this necessary first step. The wax coated glass was then taken to the needle machine. The operator carefully placed the ware upside down on a rubber cushioned plate

#207 needle etch on a #7577 Venus 9 oz. Crystal goblet. 4 3/4" high x 2" in diameter. $18-20.

#272 needle etch on a #18 Columbus decanter with a cut neck and star cut base. Crystal. Circa 1920s. 10 1/2" high. $150-175.

#345 1/2 White Gold needle etch and Platinum band decoration on a #48 Vanessa 54 oz. jug. Crystal with Jade Green handle and foot. Circa 1930s. 9" high. $450-500.

where it was held fast by suction. The operator lowered the machine's arms, each with needles fastened to one end, against the glass and turned on the machine. The glass slowly rotated while the needles traced the pattern into the wax (Bureau of Industrial Hygiene 1937-38, 38-39).

Once the pattern was inscribed in the wax, the glass was removed from the machine and a touch-up girl repaired any spots where the wax coating had been damaged by handling. Once the wax coating was repaired, the glass was taken to the to the dipping room where an acid etcher immersed the ware in a hydrofluoric acid bath. The exposed glass was eaten away by the acid, transferring the design etched in the wax to the glass. The length of time the glass was to remain in the bath was determined by the depth of the etching (Bureau of Industrial Hygiene 1937-38, 38-39).

Once the glass was removed from the bath, it was taken to a steamer. The wax was steamed off and then a polish girl polished the needle etch decorated glass with sawdust and finally with a cloth (Bureau of Industrial Hygiene 1937-38, 38-39).

Plate Etching

Before it ever appeared on a piece of glass, a plate etch design was first etched onto a steel plate. While a few glass plants etched their own plates, this job was generally handled by an outside firm (Bureau of Industrial Hygiene 1937-38, 39-40).

The transfer man, or printer, transfered the pattern from the steel plate to paper. To accomplish this, he first warmed the steel plate and placed it, design side up, on a solid table. A mixture of lamp black and melted wax was poured over the plate. Excess wax was removed with a "printer's plate," a scraper with a broad, thin, flexible steel blade. The transfer man then placed a very thin transfer paper over the plate and pressed it onto the plate with a steel roller. Before the paper was used, the side to be printed was coated with a soft soap solution so that wax would not come in direct contact with the paper. This ensured that the paper could be easily removed once the design had been transferred to the glass (Bureau of Industrial Hygiene 1937-38, 39-40).

When the transfer paper was removed from the steel plate, the wax adhered to it, leaving the design outline in the wax. That portion of the design to be etched remained wax free (Bureau of Industrial Hygiene 1937-38, 39-40).

The printed paper was taken to the print cutter who cut away the extra paper and gave the design to the "putting-on girl." The putting-on girl placed the printed side of the paper against the glassware and pressed it down smoothly by hand. The piece was then sent on to the "rubbing-down girl" who rubbed the paper with a stiff brush to ensure that every part of the design was in close contact with the glass. At that point, the "taking-off girl" removed the paper from the glass with lukewarm water, leaving the wax behind on the glass. The taking-off girl had to be care-

ful that the water was not too hot or the wax design would melt away in the bath.

From the taking-off girl, the glass went to the "touching-up girl" who covered the rest of the glass with wax, leaving only the design exposed and without any wax coating. The well-waxed glass was then sent on to the acid dipping room where it was dipped in a hydrofluoric acid bath. After that bath, the wax was removed by steaming and the now etched glass was polished with sawdust and then with a cloth (Bureau of Industrial Hygiene 1937-38, 39-40).

An advertisement from February 1936 described one of the etched designs produced by the Morgantown Glass Works as,

"Sharon," an etched design in an all-over snowflake effect brought out by the Morgantown Glass Works in full stemware, tumblers, plates, decorative pieces, and liquor glassware. A wide platinum band around the top or the rim of the article gives a finishing touch to this fine design. New stemware with a flaring bowl and a cased stem made up of close-set flat buttons are shown, too, and also a group of handsome mirtred cuttings of the old English type on two different shapes, a round-footed shape with a ball stem and a square-footed shape. ... Also new — gold floral prints on ruby stemware, plates, platters; platinum lines on Stiegel Green, Amethyst, Ritz Blue stemware with Crystal stems.

Sharon will mean a frosty crystal vogue. ... shown in the Pittsburgh Show. Its mottled frosty surface is refreshingly realistic, especially by contrast with the smart Platinum band.

Only the No. 8 Ball with matching Candlespheres are illustrated, but "Sharon" is available also in a complete line of stemware in a particularly graceful design. See this 1936 style sensation ... Prices are amazingly moderate. Morgantown Glass Works.

Three etches from the 1931 Morgantown Glass Works catalog: the Ducal, Superba, and San Toy etches.

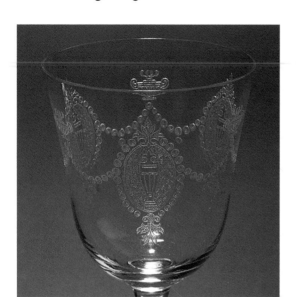

#730 Adam etch on a #7810 Monaco 9 oz. Crystal water goblet. Circa 1918. 6" high x 3 1/4" in diameter. $25-28.

#751 Adonis etch on a #7604 1/2 Heirloom 9 oz. goblet in 14K Topaz. Circa 1931. 8" high x 3 3/4" in diameter. $50-60.

#734 American Beauty etch on a #2 Arcadia 54 oz. jug without cover. Crystal. Circa 1920s. 9 1/4" high. $275-295.

Aquaria etch on a #7635 Oceana champagne. Venetian Green stem and foot with Crystal bowl. 6" high x 3 3/4" in diameter. Circa 1930s. $140-160.

#734 American Beauty etch on a #12 Crystal 8" bowl. Crystal. Circa 1920s. 5" high. $45-50.

#762 Arctic etch on a #7640 Art Moderne 9 oz. goblet. Crystal.
7 1/2" high x 3 1/2" diameter. $125-140.

Left and above: Aurora etch on a #20069 Melon vase. Crystal frosted ware dating from circa 1930s. 8 1/2" high x 6" in diameter. $1200-1500.

Below: #747 Baden etch on a 5 1/2 oz. champagne with an Ebony cased filament stem. 4 3/4" high x 4" in diameter. $95-110.

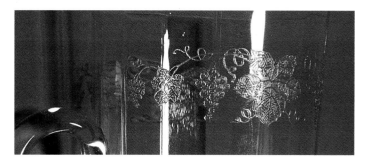

#703 Bernadette etch on a #9069 Hopper 12 oz. footed ice tea with handle. Circa 1920s. 5 1/4" high x 2 3/4" in diameter. $30-35.

#747 Biscayne etch on a #53 Serenade 10" Meadow Green vase with a Straight optic. Circa 1930s. $160-175.

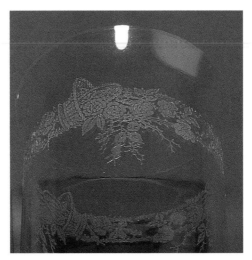

#743 Bramble Rose etch on a #9416 Topeka 10 oz. flat bottom tumbler. Crystal. Circa 1918. Straight top: 3 3/4" high x 2 1/2" in diameter. Flared top: 3 3/4" high x 2 3/4" in diameter. $20-22.

#747 Biscayne etch on a #7620 Fontanne 9 oz. goblet. Crystal bowl and foot; Ebony cased filament stem. 7 3/4" high x 3 1/2" in diameter. $125-150

Carlton etch decoration on a #21 Dominion 12" frosty punch bowl, shown with #7023 cog base 5 oz. punch cups. Bowl: 12" high x 12" diameter. Cups: 4 1/2" high x 2 3/4" diameter. Circa 1920s. $1800-2000.

#743 Bramble Rose etch on a #23 Karma 32 oz jug without a cover. Crystal. Circa 1920s. 7 1/4" high. $225-250.

#778 Carlton Madrid etch on a #7665 Laura 9 oz. goblet. 14K Topaz bowl with Crystal stem and foot. Circa 1931. 8 1/4" high x 3 1/2" in diameter. $75-85.

#784 Carleton "Marco" etch on a #37 Barry 48 oz jug. Crystal. Platinum encrusted #31 band. Circa 1931. 9 1/2" high x 6 1/2" in diameter. $395-425.

#757 Elizabeth etch on a #7664 Queen Anne 10 oz. goblet. Crystal. Circa 1931. 8 1/2" high x 3 1/4" in diameter. $75-85.

#811 Cathay etch on a #7711 Callahan 9 oz. Crystal goblet. Circa 1950s. 7 1/2" high x 3 1/2" in diameter. $30-35.

#790 Fairwin etch on a #7673 Lexington footed goblet. Ritz Blue cased filament stem. Circa 1931. 6 1/4" high x 3 1/4" in diameter. $95-110.

#798 Eileen etch on a #7673 Lexington goblet with Gold band decoration. 7 1/2" high x 2 3/4" diameter. Circa 1930s. $75-85.

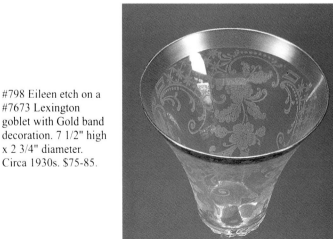

#790 Fairwin etch on a #7673 Lexington 5 1/2 oz. saucer champagne. Ritz Blue cased filament stem. Circa 1931. 6 1/2" high x 4" in diameter. $90-100.

Faun etch on a #7640 Art Moderne 5 1/2 oz. champagne. Cryatal bowl and foot; Ebony stem. Circa 1931. 5 1/2" high x 4 1/4" in diameter. $115-125.

#796 Floret etch on a #7684 Yale luncheon goblet. Ritz Blue cased filament stem. Circa 1932. 6" high x 3 1/2" in diameter. $175-195.

#785 Fernlee etch on a #9074 Belton Crystal tumbler. Circa 1930s. 5" high x 3 3/4" in diameter. $40-45.

#781 Fontinelle etch on a #7620 Fontanne 9 oz goblet. Meadow Green bowl, Crystal stem and foot. Circa 1931. 7 1/2" high x 3 1/2" in diameter. $175-195.

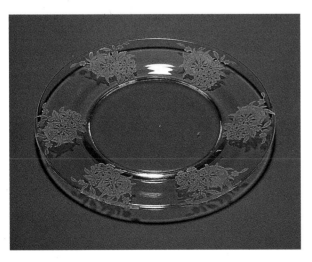

#796 Floret etch on a #1511 round Crystal plate. Circa 1930s. 7 1/2" in diameter. $15-18.

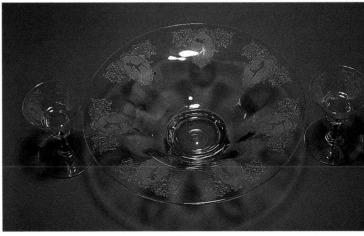

#781 Fontinelle etch on a #4355 Janice 13" console bowl. Crystal. 13" in diameter. $395-425. This console bowl is accompanied by a pair of #7620 Fontanne 4 3/4" low candlesticks. Ebony cased filament stem. #781 Fontinelle etch. 4 3/4" high x 3 1/2" in diameter. $300-350.

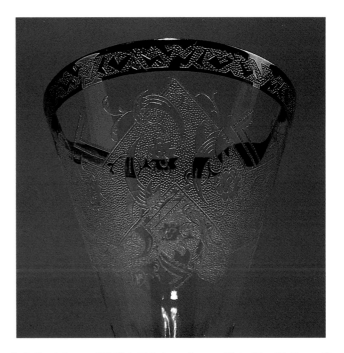

Labelle etch on a #7640 Art Moderne 9 oz. goblet with a Platinum #3 band. All Crystal.7 1/2" high x 3 1/2" in diameter. $125-145.

Hunt scene etch in Silver on a #10 1/2 Lynward Ebony decanter with a Crystal octogan stopper. 11" high. Circa 1930s. $400-450.

Labelle etch with a #3 Platinum band on a #7640 Art Moderne 9 oz. goblet. Crystal bowl and foot. Ebony stem. 7 3/4" high x 3 1/2" in diameter. $125-150.

#760 Kyoto etch on a #7634 Tiburon 9 oz. goblet. Venetian Green stem and foot. 7 3/4" high x 3 1/4" in diameter. $70-80.

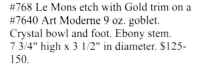

#768 Le Mons etch with Gold trim on a #7640 Art Moderne 9 oz. goblet. Crystal bowl and foot. Ebony stem. 7 3/4" high x 3 1/2" in diameter. $125-150.

Lotus etch on a #7654 Lorna 9 oz. Crystal goblet. Circa 1930s. 8 1/4" high x 3 1/4" in diameter. $50-60.

#763 Marilyn etch on a #7636 Square 5 1/2 oz. champagne. Anna Rose stem and foot. Circa 1929. 7" high x 4" in diameter. $180-200.

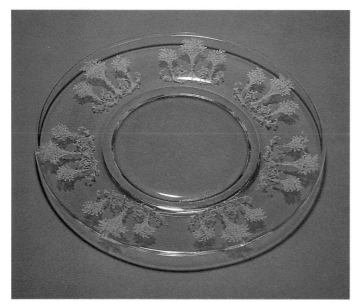

#787 Maytime etch on a #7675 Paula 5 1/2 oz. champagne. Ritz Blue cased filament stem. Crystal bowl and foot. Circa 1931. 6 1/2" high x 4" in diameter. $85-95.

#808 Mikado etch with a #29 border on a #37 Barry Spanish Red 48oz. jug with Venetia painted Gold decoration. 8 1/2" high to lip. $500-550.

#766 Nantucket etch on a #7654 Lorna Crystal footed tumbler with a Panel optic. 6" high x 3 1/2" diameter. Circa 1930s. $45-50.

#787 1/2 Mayfair etch on a #1511 round Crystal plate. Circa 1930s. 7 1/2" in diameter. $15-18.

#766 Nantucket etch on a #7654 Lorna champagne. Venetian Green stem and foot. Circa 1931. 6 1/2" high x 3 3/4" in diameter. $80-90.

Picardy etch on a #7646 Sophisticate 9 oz. goblet. Circa 1920s. 7" high x 4" in diameter. $25-30.

#776 Nasreen etch on a #7606 1/2 Athena 9 oz. goblet. Ebony cased filament stem. Circa 1931. 7 1/2" high x 3 3/4" in diameter. $85-95.

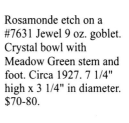

Rosamonde etch on a #7631 Jewel 9 oz. goblet. Crystal bowl with Meadow Green stem and foot. Circa 1927. 7 1/4" high x 3 1/4" in diameter. $70-80.

#705 Pembrooke Poppy etch on a #12 Viola vase, Crystal. 6" high x 6" diameter. Circa 1920s. $95-115.

Saranac etch on a #7690 Monroe 9 oz. goblet. Circa 1932. 8 1/2" high x 3 3/4" in diameter. $50-55.

#749 Shamrock etch on a #1 Cadenza 24 oz. cocktail server. Circa 1923. Removable top. 10" high. $190-210.

#769 Platinum Sparta etch on a #9051 Zenith Ritz Blue 1 1/2 oz. bar tumbler. $95-115.

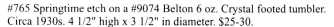

#765 Springtime etch on a #9074 Belton 6 oz. Crystal footed tumbler. Circa 1930s. 4 1/2" high x 3 1/2" in diameter. $25-30.

#758 Sunrise Medallion etch on a #45 Catherine 10" vase. Meadow Green. Circa 1931. 10" high. $200-225.

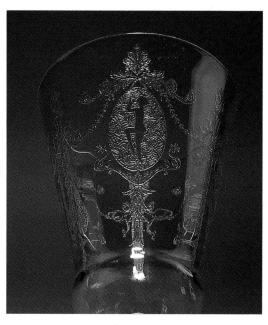

#758 Sunrise Medallion etch on a #7664 Queen Anne 10 oz. goblet in the Anna Rose color. Circa 1931. 8 1/2" high x 3 1/4" in diameter. $95-110.

Superba etch on a #7654 1/2 Legacy 9 oz. Crystal goblet with an Ebony cased filament stem. Circa 1931. 8" high x 3 1/2" in diameter. $175-195.

Left and below: Superba etch on a #7664 Queen Anne 6 1/2 oz. Crystal champagne. Circa 1931. 8" high x 4" in diameter. $175-195.

#795 Versailles etch on a #7711 Callahan 9 oz. Crystal goblet. Circa 1950s. 7 3/4" high x 3 1/2" in diameter. $25-30.

#756 Tinkerbell etch on a #7631 Jewel 9 oz. goblet. Azure Blue. Circa 1927. 7 1/2" high x 2 3/4" in diameter. $125-140.

#727 Victoria etch on a #20 Brompton Crystal bowl (in the center). Circa 1920. 5 3/4" high x 7 1/2" in diameter. $125-150. Left: 3 oz #7586 "Napa" Cocktail. #727 Victoria etch. Circa 1920. 4" high x 3" in diameter. $25-28. Right: Ice cream dish, line 300. #727 Victoria etch. Circa 1920. 3" high x 4" in diameter. $20-25.

#727 Victoria Regina etch (combined with a floral cutting—to clarify: the etch and cut combination was identified as Victoria Regina) on a #7640 Art Moderne 9 oz. goblet. Circa 1931. Crystal bowl and foot. India black stem. Circa 1931. 7 1/2" high x 3" in diameter. $125-140.

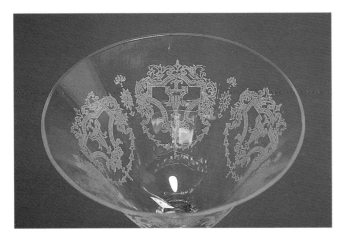

#733 Virginia etch on a #7711 Callahan champagne and sherbet. Circa 1920. Crystal. Champagne: 6" high x 4" in diameter. Crystal. Sherbet: 4 1/2" high x 4" in diameter. $18-20 each.

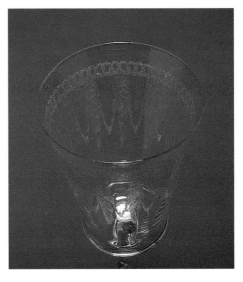

A Woodland etch on a #7664 Queen Anne 10 oz. goblet. Azure Blue. Circa 1931. 8 1/2" high x 3 1/4" in diameter. $75-85.

#733 Virginia etch on a #23 Karma 54oz Crystal jug with cover. Circa 1920. 7 1/4" high. $295-325.

Encrustation

When speaking of Morgantown glass decoration, any etch over which enamel has been painted is referred to as an "encrustation." Once the etch was overpainted with the enamel, it was fired to finish the glass (Wiley 1997, 2-3).

Frosting

A frosted glass effect was created by dipping crystal blanks into a bath of hydroflouric acid (Wiley 1997, 2-3).

#758 Sunrise Medallion enamel and Gold encrusted etch on a #7606 Hopemont tumbler 3 1/8" diameter x 4 1/4" high Crystal iridized body with 2-Disc Anna Rose base. Circa 1930s. $200-250.

A mottled frosted surface decoration on a Crystal #8 Luna ball vase. 7" high. Circa 1930s. $140-160.

Ice Decoration

To create an "ice effect," a layer of printing oil or a mixture of balsam or copaiba and turpentine was applied to the glass with a rubber stamp or brush. When this oil or mixture became tacky, glass "ice" was poured over the impression and a layer of it adhered to the surface. The "ice" itself was a colored or colorless low melting granu-

lar glass that was crushed and screened to 50-150 mesh size. Once the ice was in place, the piece was fired. If the applied ice was underfired, the ice was sharp and rough; if it was overfired, the ice effect was completely lost (Bureau of Industrial Hygiene 1937-38, 41).

Luster Decoration

Striking iridescent effects were created on glass with lusters. Lusters are metallic resinates dissolved in a solvent such as lavender oil. Colorless lusters give a mother-of-pearl effect and colored lusters produce an iridescent and colored metallic sheen. Luster was applied to completely clean and thoroughly dry glassware either in a spray or with a brush. Moisture on the glass would cause white spots on the fired ware (Bureau of Industrial Hygiene 1937-38, 43).

Glassware sprayed or brushed with luster had to be allowed to dry completely before it was fired and lehr ports had to be left open to allow evaporating oils to escape (Bureau of Industrial Hygiene 1937-38, 43).

Gold iridescent decorated Crystal sugar and creamer. Sugar: 3" high x 4 1/2" diameter. Creamer: 4" high. Circa 1920s. $175-200 set.

Metallic Decorations

Gold, silver, and platinum were all applied to glassware in addition to vitrified colors and lusters. There were two types of metallic decoration, bright and burnished. Burnished metals were generally supplied by manufacturers in a paste form and applied with a brush. After firing, the metal was burnished using burnishing sand, a fine round grained sand that would not scratch the metal (Bureau of Industrial Hygiene 1937-38, 44).

The bright metal was a resinate dissolved in turpentine and lavender oil, containing a small amount of rhodium that caused the metal to turn bright when fired. This eliminated the need for burnishing. As with the burnished metal, this resinate mix was applied with a brush (Bureau of Industrial Hygiene 1937-38, 44).

Electroplating was also used to produce fine decorative effects. Electroplated designs were first printed and fired onto the glass with a paste mixture containing precipitating silver flux and oil. All of the disparate parts of the decoration were connected with an electric current source, the ware was immersed in an electroplating bath, and a deposit of pure silver was plated over the fired design. This was polished and frequently given a coating of rhodium to prevent tarnishing (Bureau of Industrial Hygiene 1937-38, 44).

Platinum floral and Platinum bands decorations on a #10 1/2 Lynward decander with a Crystal octagon stopper. Ritz Blue. 11 1/4" high. Circa 1930s. $400-450.

Gold banded rim and foot decoration on three tumblers. From left: #9401 Patterson 9 oz. tumbler, 5" high; #9401 Patterson 5 oz. tumbler, 3 1/2" high; #9074 Belton 2 1/2 oz.. tumbler, 3 1/4" high. All in 14K Topaz with the #733 Virginia etch. Circa 1920s. $35-40 each.

Silver decoration on a #4355 Janice 13" console bowl with a rolled rim. Ritz Blue. Circa 1930s. $300-350.

Rubber Stamp Decoration

This was a simple decorating technique in which a small amount of printing oil was first spread onto a glass plate with a rubber roller. Once the oil was spread out into a thin film, a rubber stamp with a design cut into it was then used to transfer the printing oil from the glass plate to the glassware to be decorated. When the transfered oil became tacky, the desired color was dusted onto the ware and rubbed into the oil with a cotton wad (Bureau of Industrial Hygiene 1937-38, 41).

Silk Screen Decoration and Its Precursor, Steel Plate Transfers

Steel Plate Transfers

The steel plate transfer method was replaced with silk screen techniques which were faster and less labor-intensive. In steel plate transfers, the steel plate to be etched was first coated with a plastic-like mixture of asphaltum varnish and beeswax. Once this varnish coating was hard enough to be handled, the design was cut onto the varnish, exposing the steel plate below. Dilute nitric acid was poured onto the plate and allowed to stand until the proper etch depth had been achieved. Most plants had a photo-engraving company handle this job for them (Bureau of Industrial Hygiene 1937-38, 42-43).

The print color was then finely ground and mixed with a heavy printing oil or with varnish. There was a drawback to using varnish, it became so stiff that it had to be heated before it could be used. The etching plate was heated and warm color was spread over it. Excess color was removed with a printers plate scraper. In fact, the plate was scraped until very little color remained visible. The paper used to transfer the color pattern was again a special thin

stock, one side treated with a soft soap solution as before to prevent color from coming into direct contact with the paper (Bureau of Industrial Hygiene 1937-38, 42-43).

In the printing process, the paper was placed on the plate with the treated side down. A heavy felt blanket was placed over the paper and the plate was run through a press. The paper then had to be dried out before it could be removed from the plate. Ususually the drying process was accelerated with either hot air or a gas jet (Bureau of Industrial Hygiene 1937-38, 42-43).

The paper holding the pattern to be transferred was then sent to the cutting girl who cut away all of the unprinted paper. The transfer girl took the printed paper and placed it, printed side down, onto the glass. A helper, using a stiff brush, rubbed the design until it was in complete contact with the glass. The paper was then removed from the ware by immersing it in lukewarm water. At that point, the pattern was successfully transferred (Bureau of Industrial Hygiene 1937-38, 42-43).

Silk Screen Decoration

In 1939, the silk screen process was rapidly replacing the steel plate transfer process. Simply put, silk screening was a stenciling process that involved forcing colored material onto a glass blank through meshes made of either silk or organdy screen. The screen was prepared in such a way that previously printed areas and areas not to receive any color were impervious to the colored material (Wiley 1997, 2-3).

Queen Louise silk screen decoration on a #7617 Hampton cocktail, 2 1/2 oz. Anna Rose foot and base. Crystal bowl. Circa 1928. 5" high x 3" in diameter. $125-150.

Manchester Pheasant silk screen decoration on a #7664 Queen Anne 10 oz. goblet. 8 1/2" high x 3 1/2" diameter. Circa 1930s. $195-225.

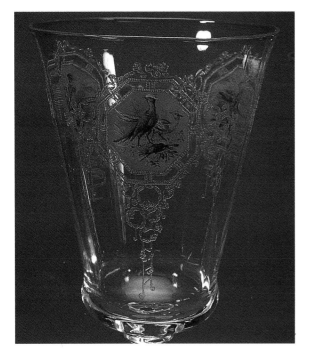

To create the silk screen, a piece of fine bolting cloth measuring around 150 meshes to the linear inch was stretched tightly and mounted on a hard wood or plywood frame. The cloth itself was permeable to color paste and fluids of a high consistency and had to be made impermeable with specific chemicals. Colors passed through the unprotected portions and the screen acted as a negative for printing (Bureau of Industrial Hygiene 1937-38, 46-49).

Two methods for preparing the silk screen were in use in 1939. One method involved cutting the design onto an acetate sheet and then fixing this sheet to the screen. The other was a photographic method (Bureau of Industrial Hygiene 1937-38, 46-49).

Using the acetate sheet method, the portion of the design which was colored was removed. The sheet was laid on a flat surface and the stretched screen was laid over it. A solvent was then applied to the sheet and screen to fix the acetate to the silk screen (Bureau of Industrial Hygiene 1937-38, 46-49).

To print colors onto glass from the screen, the silk screen was held against the glass and color paste was rubbed through the screen. This was usually done by a machine that slowly rotated the glassware as the screen moved over it. It was essential that the glassware and the screen moved at the same speed to avoid smearing the design. A separate screen was needed for each color in the design. Metallic oxides and vitrous color pastes were used for this printing process (Bureau of Industrial Hygiene 1937-38, 46-49).

After the screeners had printed the glassware, wipers removed any smears found on the glass with kerosene dampened rags. At this point, colors were allowed to dry and the ware was then fired (Bureau of Industrial Hygiene 1937-38, 46-49).

In the photographic method, the cloth was covered twice with a sensitizing solution (two coatings ensured that there would be no pinholes or similar defects). When exposed to light, this solution set or became insoluable to a solution that was used to wash out the unexposed portion (Bureau of Industrial Hygiene 1937-38, 46-49).

The design to be produced on the screen was traced onto tracing paper or onto a glass plate in opaque ink. A glass plate provided the best results but was more difficult to trace the design upon (Bureau of Industrial Hygiene 1937-38, 46-49).

To expose the design, one side of the screen was covered with a felt pad to eliminate light leakage from behind. Then the tracing or glass plate was placed on the screen so that it was in complete contact with the screen and both were exposed to a strong light (Bureau of Industrial Hygiene 1937-38, 46-49).

As with all photographic processes, the light made the exposed ammonium bichromate gum coating insoluable to water while the unexposed portion which the inked design protected from the light could be dissolved in a mild stream of lukewarm water. The remaining coat was hardened by immersion in a chemical bath for five minutes (Bureau of Industrial Hygiene 1937-38, 46-49).

Skilled lehr operators were required to fire silk screen decorated glassware. The lehr itself needed to be well ventilated to allow volatile oils to escape and to prevent moisture from damaging the enamel. Moisture could wreak havoc on a silk screen design, causing it to blister during firing (Bureau of Industrial Hygiene 1937-38, 46-49).

The Queen Louise silk screen decoration was produced by the Economy Glass Company. The trade journal *China, Glass and Lamp* reported upon the arrival of this line on April 2, 1928, stating that the design had been produced on a line of stemware first introduced at the Pittsburgh Glass Exhibition in January. The striking Queen Louise decoration is surrounded by an etched and frosted medallion which frames the colorful silk screen portrait of its namesake. The etched and frosted medallion was applied to the glass first and then the silk screen pattern was placed over it (Gallagher 1990, 39-40).

Staining

At times the Morgantown factory would apply a thin layer of a different colored glass over a piece of glassware to finish the product. This is referred to as staining (Wiley 1997, 2-3).

Decorations Within the Glass

We have discussed surface decorating techniques ranging from applied rims to glass staining. Now we will move inward, discussing decorations that are either molded into the body of the glass or that take place within the body of the glass. There are three decorative techniques to be discussed.

Optics, Decorations From the Mold

As previously discussed, an optic is a decoration molded into the body of the glassware. The decoration is transferred from the interior of the two piece mold, where it was originally carved, to the body of the ware as the hot blown glass expanded to fill the interior of the mold.

Palm optic on an assortment of #7673 Lexington Ritz Blue cased filament stemwares with Crystal bowls and feet. Circa 1931. Back left: 9 oz. goblet, 7 3/4" high x 4" in diameter, $85-95; back right: 5 1/2 oz. saucer champagne, 6 1/2" high x 4" in diameter, $75-85; Front left: 3 1/2 oz. cocktail, 5" high x 3"across, $65-75; front right: 5 1/2 oz. sherbet, 4" high x 4" in diameter, $65-75.

Look closely for the Panel optic on a #7654 Lorna Crystal footed tumbler with a #766 Nantucket etch. 6" high x 3 1/2" diameter. Circa 1930s. $45-50.

Below: Peacock optic on a #9921 Delphine Flowerlite with a Crystal flower frog. Evergreen color. Circa 1958. 4 1/2" high x 3" in diameter. $35-40.

Pineapple optic on an institutional ware syrup pitcher. Crystal with an Amber foot. Circa 1940s. 5 1/2" high. $30-35.

Pin/Spiral optic on a #12 Viola 8" vase in Venetian Green with Gold decoration. Circa 1920s. 8" high. $70-80.

Spiral optic on a #18 Lynda 8" vase. Thistle color. Circa 1962. 8" high x 3 1/2" in diameter at top. $45-50.

Prior to 1937, optics appearing on Morgantown glass included the Cascade, Festoon, Palm, Peacock, Pineapple, Pillar, and Tulip. After 1937, the Guild produced the Spiral optic. When the Spiral optic mold was discontinued in 1963, it was retooled by the company to create a line of textured tableware in 1966 known as Festival. The Festival line had a short two year run and was produced in Crystal, Amber, Gloria Blue, and Moss Green colors (Gallagher 1995, 62, 207). During the Guild years, the company also produced a number of unusual glass shapes, textures, and effects that will be seen in Chapter 4. All The Wares.

When the Spiral optic mold was discontinued in 1963, it was retooled by the company to create a line of textured tableware in 1966 known as Festival. #3000 Festival 7 1/2" plate in Gloria Blue and the #3000 Festival berry bowl in Gloria Blue. 2 1/2" high x 3 1/2" diameter. Circa 1960s. Plate: $8-12; berry bowl: $12-15.

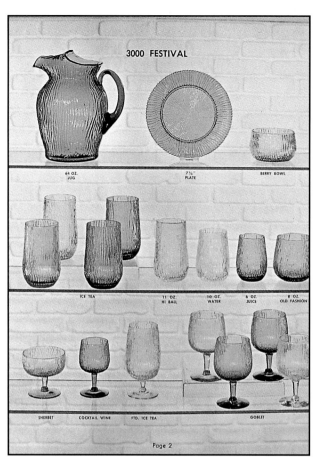

The #3000 Festival line.

Cased Filament Stemware

Cased filament stems were a Morgantown original first presented to the public in 1935. Cased filament stems feature a thin central core of color surrounded by a pressed crystal clear glass stem. Cased filament stem colors include Black, Green, Ritz Blue, and Spanish Red.

Below: Institutional glass with cased filament stems in Ritz Blue, Steigel Green, Spanish Red, and Ebony. All but one of the bowls are Crystal in color.

Formal glassware with cased filament stems in Ebony, Ritz Blue, and Spanish Red.

To create the colorful cased stem, the desired color destined to end up in the center of the stem was placed in the press well first. Then crystal glass was placed on top of the color and the mold was placed over top of the press well and the blown bowl was set on top of the press mold. At that point in the process, the presser depressed the handle that pushed the plunger which pressed the glass up into the stem (Brivtec 1993, 7).

Colored glass was a little harder by nature than Crystal glass. This was one of the reasons the color pressed up into the center of the Crystal. The other reason was that the colored glass, dropped into the press well first, cooled more quickly and would shoot up in the center of the hotter Crystal when the plunger was pushing the glass (Brivtec 1993, 7).

Controlled Bubbles

This neat little effect gave the impression that bubbles of various sizes swirled up through glass connectors or finials. The effect was created by piercing the connector or finial with a particular pattern when that piece was still in its molten state. This created tiny air pockets that appeared as swirling bubbles when the glass cooled.

The controlled bubble decorative technique is shown in the Crystal stem of this #7955 Universal 12" flower bowl, in India Black with a Crystal stem and foot. Circa 1930s. $350-400.

Chapter 4. All The Wares

The Formative & the Elegant Years, 1899-1937

As there is very little photographed here that dates to the earliest years of Morgantown production, the first two periods have been combined. The major categories into which the glasswares have been divided are those categories created by the company management over the years of production.

Among collectors, the very best of the baskets, console bowls, and vases (many with Italian bases), produced from the late 1920s to 1937 are commonly referred to as the "Continental Line (Gallagher 1995, 39)." This refers

to the fact that the decorative techniques used on these exceptional pieces originated in Continental Europe and were brought to Morgantown by skilled immigrant artisans. While this was not a name used by the company to identify their wares, it is a term one should be familiar with.

#19 Orlando 7" basket in Old Amethyst with Crystal applied rim and Crystal twisted reed handle. Circa 1930s. $750-795.

Baskets

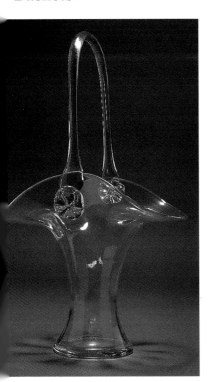

#19 Orlando basket. Crystal. Circa 1920. 12 3/4" high. $175-225.

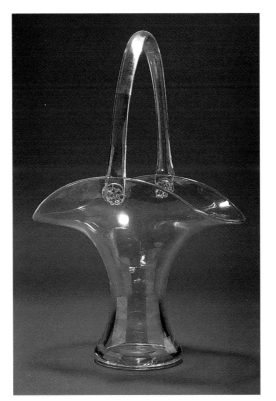

#19 Orlando basket. Rainbow (iridized). Circa 1920. 12" high. $175-225.

#19 Orlando basket. Old Amethyst with an applied Crystal rim and Crystal twisted reed handle. 11 1/4" in diameter, 15 1/2" high. $850-900.

#19-4358 Patrick 8" Crystal flower basket, crimped rim and twisted reed handle. Circa 1930s. $550-600.

#19-4358 Patrick 8" Ritz Blue flower basket with Crystal twisted reed handle. Circa 1930s. 13" high. $650-700.

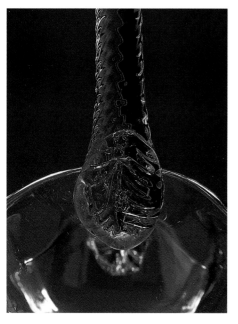

Close-up of the leaf decoration on the #19-4358 Patrick flower basket.

#19-4358 Patrick 10" Spanish Red flower basket with Crystal twisted reed handle. Circa 1930s. 16 1/4" high. $700-750.

#19-4358 Patrick baskets (6" and 5") in Stiegel Green with Crystal twisted reed handles. Circa 1930s. $650-700.

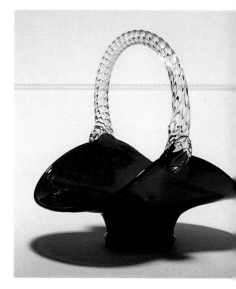

#20 Jennie 4 1/4" Ritz Blue bon bon basket with a Crystal reed handle. Circa 1930s. 8 3/4" high. $650-700.

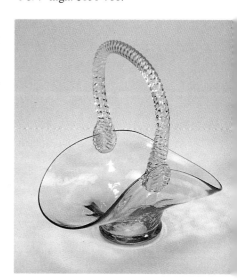

#20 Jennie 4 1/4" bon bon basket in Anna Rose with Peacock optic and Crystal reed handle. 7 1/2" lip to lip and 7 1/2" high. Circa 1930s. $650-700.

#20 Jennie 4 1/2" Old Amethyst bon bon basket with a Crystal twisted reed handle. $650-700.

#20 Jennie 4 1/2" Stiegel Green bon bon basket with Crystal reed handle. Circa 1930s. 8 1/2" high. 7.5" in diameter length. $650-700.

#4356 Irene 10 1/2" bowl-shaped basket in Stiegel Green with applied Crystal rim. Crystal twisted reed handle. Circa 1920s. 11" high x 10 1/2" in diameter at widest point. $825-875.

#4357 Trindle 9" Spanish Red flower basket with six crimped rim. Crystal reed handle. Circa 1930s. $650-700.

#4357 Trindle 9" Old Amethyst flower basket with a crimped rim and a Crystal twisted reed handle. Circa 1930s. $700-750.

#36-4354 Ashley 10" flower basket in Ritz Blue with Crystal foot and twisted reed handle. Circa 1930s. $775-850.

Left: #36-4354 Ashely 10" flower basket. Old Amethyst with Crystal foot and twisted Crystal reed handle. Circa 1930s. $775-850.

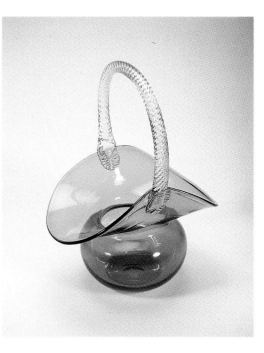

Right: #4357 1/2 Clayton 10" Golden Iris basket with a "canoe shaped rim" and a Crystal applied reed handle. Circa 1930s. $650-700.

#4357 1/2 Clayton 10" Ebony basket with a canoe shape rim and an applied twisted Crystal reed handle. Circa 1930s. $725-800.

Bitter Bottles

8 Parsons bitter bottles. Crystal with red band Hollywood decoration (satin frosting on bottom with applied glossy red and band of bright Platinum on top). Shown with a matching ice tub. Bottles: 4 3/4" high. Tub: 4" high x 6" diameter. Circa 1930s. Bottles: $125-150 each; tub: $150-175.

#4357 1/2 Clayton 10" Ritz Blue basket with a canoe shaped rim and a Crystal twisted reed handle. Circa 1930s. $650-700.

Bon Bons with Covers

#16 Rachel 5" covered bon bon. Crystal with Pandora cutting. Circa 1920s. $225-250.

#2938 Helga bon bon in Stiegel Green with a Crystal Golf Ball knob. 4 1/2" high x 4 1/2" in diameter. Circa 1930s. $400-450.

Below: #9074 Maureen bon bon dish in Ritz Blue with a Crystal base and Golf Ball knob on a #2 cover. 6" high, 4 1/2" in diameter. Circa 1930s. $350-395.

#2938 Helga bon bon in Ritz Blue with Platinum band decoration and a Golf Ball knob. 5 1/4" high x 5 1/4" in diameter. Circa 1930s. $400-450.

#14 Fairlee 8" Two-Tone Genova bowl. Circa 1920s. 6" high. (This bowl comes with a cover and without.) $225-250.

#9074 Maureen bon bon in Spanish Red with a Crystal base and Golf Ball knob on a #2 cover. 5 1/4" high x 4 1/2" in diameter. Circa 1930s. $400-450.

Bowls

#19 Kelsha 12" diameter bowl in Nanking Blue. Circa 1920s. $300-350.

Spittoon bowl in Ritz Blue. 6" high x 7 3/4" diameter. Circa 1920s. $350-400.

#12 Crystal 8" bowl. Crystal with #734 American Beauty etch. Circa 1920s. 5" high. $45-50.

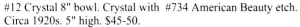

#19 Kelsha 12" bowl. Two-Tone Danube. Grape cutting. Circa 1921. 8" high x 12 1/2" in diameter. $350-375.

#19 Kelsha 12" bowl. Two-Tone Danube. Lydia cutting. Circa 1921. 7 1/2" high x 12 1/2" in diameter. $350-375.

#20 Brompton bowl (in center), Crystal decorated with the #727 Victoria etch. Circa 1920. 5 3/4" high x 7 1/2" in diameter. $125-150. This bowl is accompanied by *left:* #7586 "Napa" 3 oz. Cocktail. #727 Victoria etch. Circa 1920. 4" high x 3" in diameter. $25-28 and *right:* #300 ice cream dish. #727 Victoria etch. Circa 1920. 3" high x 4" in diameter. $20-25.

#21 Dominion 12" punch bowl, frosty Carlton etch decoration, shown with #7023 cog base 5 oz. punch cups. Bowl: 12" high x 12" diameter. Cups: 4 1/2" high x 2 3/4" diameter. Circa 1920s. $1800-2000.

#26 Greer Two-Tone Neubian 10" bowl.
Circa 1920s. 4.5" high. $395-425.

#35 1/2 Elena 9 1/2" compote bowl, crimped, in
Old Bristol. Circa 1930s. $650-700.

#27 Edna bowl in Ritz Blue. 13 1/2" diameter.
Circa 1920s. $350-400.

#71 Vienna 12" diameter Stiegel Green
console bowl with Crystal Italian base. Circa
1930s. $750-850.

#35 1/2 Elena 9 1/2" compote bowl, Ritz
Blue, crimped, with Crystal base. Circa
1930s. $200-250.

#4355 Janice 11"
rolled rim Ritz
Blue console
bowl. Circa
1930s. 11" in
diameter. $150-
185.

#4355 Janice 13" console bowl. Crystal with #781 Fontinelle etch. 13" in diameter. $395-425. The console bowl is shown with a pair of #7620 Fontanne 4 3/4" low candlesticks with Ebony cased filament stem. The candlesticks are also decorated with the #781 Fontinelle etch. 4 3/4" high x 3 1/2" in diameter. $300-350.

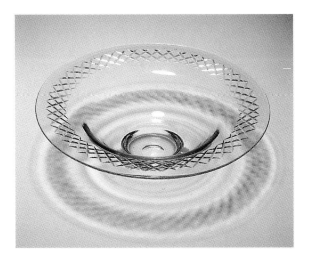

#4355 Janice 13" Crystal console bowl with unknown cutting. Circa 1930s. $150-175.

#4355 Janice 13" console bowl in Jade with Palm optic. Circa 1930s. $450-495.

#4355 Janice 13" Ritz Blue console bowl. Circa 1930s. $150-185.

#4355 Janice Crystal 13" console bowl,
Duo-tone with Randall Blue rolled rim.
Circa 1930s. $150-185.

#4355 Janice 13" Old Bristol Line console
bowl. Ritz Blue with Alabaster trim. Circa
1930s. 13" in diameter. $600-650.

#4355 Janice 13" Ritz Blue console bowl
with applied Crystal rim. Circa 1930s. 13" in
diameter. $375-425.

#4355 Janice 13" Ritz Blue console
bowl with applied #769 Platinum
Sparta etch. Circa 1930s. $375-425.

#4355 Janice 13" console bowl with rolled
rim. Ritz Blue with Silver decoration. Circa
1930s. $300-350.

#7801 grapefruit bowl without the liner.
Crystal with a #737 Adam etch. 3 1/2" high
x 4 1/2" diameter. Circa pre-1920s. $60-70.

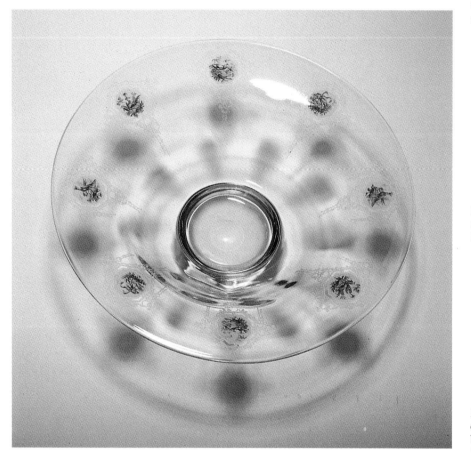

Left: #4355 13" Crystal console bowl with
duotone silkscreening in Manchester
Pheasant design. Circa 1930s. $1500-1800.

Below: #7955 Universal flower bowl with
controlled bubble Crystal stem. India black
bowl. 12" in diameter, 5 3/4" high. Circa
1930s. $350-395.

#4355 Janice 13", 8-
crimp Spanish Red
console bowl. Circa
1930s. $175-195.

Candlesticks

In 1935, Torch Candles were offered in Crystal, Stiegel Green with a crystal stem, Ritz Blue with a crystal stem, and Ruby with a crystal stem, each for fifty cents retail. These candle holders were described as "... long largely confined to use in connection with solemn ceremonies, [Torch Candles] are now interesting to hostesses as an adjunct to dining. ... after the meal the 'torches' go to the living room to be used as lighters or to furnish a decorative note (*Turnover Topics* 1935, 9).

#7660 Empire 6 3/4" Ritz Blue torch candle with Crystal stem and foot. Circa 1930s. 2.75" diameter bowl. $300-350 pair.

Pair of Crystal candlesticks with twist stem. Circa 1931. 4 1/4 " high x 3" in diameter. $295-325.

#1 Bristol 3 5/8" Old Bristol line candleholder. Ritz Bowl bowl and foot with an Alabaster stem. Circa 1930s. 3" in diameter. $550-650.

#8 Mars candleholders and #8 Luna ball vase in Old Amethyst. $250-275 set.

#37 Emperor 8" candleholder vase in Genova. Circa 1920s. $250-290 pair.

#37 Emperor 12" candleholder vase. Danube (Crystal with Nanking Blue foot). Flower cutting. 12" high. $200-220 pair.

#37 Emperor 10" candleholder vase in Crystal with unknown cutting. Circa 1920s. 10" high. $225-250 pair.

#37 Emperor 12" candleholder vase. Two-Tone Genova trim with four unidentified floral etchs, including the etch on the foot. An "S" appears on the base of the foot as well. Circa 1920s. $425-475 pair.

#7640 Art Moderne low candlesticks in Ebony. Crystal stem and foot. 4" high. Circa 1930s. $325-350.

#1933 LMX (El Mexicano) 4" candleholder vase in Seaweed. Circa 1930s. $250-275 pair.

Pair of #7620 Fontanne 4 3/4" low candlesticks. Ebony cased filament stem. #781 Fontinelle etch. 4 3/4" high x 3 1/2" in diameter. $300-350.

#7640 Art Moderne low candlestick in Meadow Green with Crystal foot and stem. 4 1/4" high. Circa 1930s. $325-350 pair.

#7640 Art Moderne 4 1/4" Ritz Blue with Crystal stem and foot low candlestick. Circa 1930s. $325-350 pair.

#7640 Art Moderne 4 1/4" low candlestick. Crystal bowl and foot. Ebony stem. 4 1/4" high x 3" in diameter. Circa 1931. $325-350 pair.

#7643 Dupont Golf Ball 4 5/8" low candlestick in Spanish Red with Crystal stem and foot. Circa 1930s. $275-325 pair.

#7643 Golf Ball 6" torch candles. Spanish red with Crystal stem and foot. Circa 1930s. $325-375 pair.

#7653 candlesticks. Crystal with a #784 Carlton Marco etch and a Platinum encrusted # 31 band. 5 1/2" high x 3 1/2" diameter. Circa 1930s. $300-350 pair.

#7643 Jacobi 4" Crystal candleholder. Circa 1931. 4" high x 3" in diameter. $175-195 pair.

#7643 Jacobi 4" Crystal candleholder with floral cutting. Circa 1931. 4" high x 3" in diameter. $250-275 pair.

#7660 Empire 8" high candlesticks. Left: Ritz Blue with Crystal stem and foot. Right: Meadow Green with Crystal stem and foot and Panel optic. 3 1/2" in diameter. Circa 1930s. Left: $350-400 pair; right: $300-350 pair.

#7951 Stafford 3 1/8" high x 4 5/8" wide candleholders in Anna Rose with #734 American Beauty etch. Circa 1930s. $500-550.

Right: #7950 Campbell candleholder in Two-Tone Laurel line. 10 1/4" high. Circa 1920s. $450-500 pair.

Pair of #7662 Majesty 4" low candlesticks. 14K Topaz bowl; Crystal foot. Circa 1931. 4" high x 3 1/2" in diameter. $325-350.

#7688 1/2 Roanoke candlestick with a #795 Versailles etch and Platinum band. 4 3/4" high x 3 1/2" in diameter. $300-350 pair.

Boxes and Jars with Covers

#15 1/2 Lisbon candy jar. Crystal with #2 cover. #734 American Beauty etch. Circa 1920s. 6 1/2" high. $195-225.

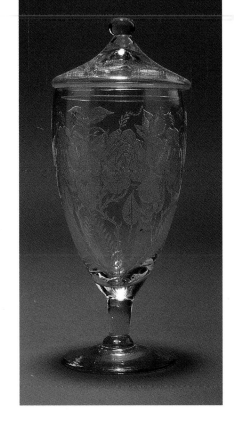

#14 Guilford 22 oz. candy jar with #3 cover in Two-Tone Danube with an unknown cutting. 11" high x 4 1/2" in diameter. Circa 1930s. $250-275.

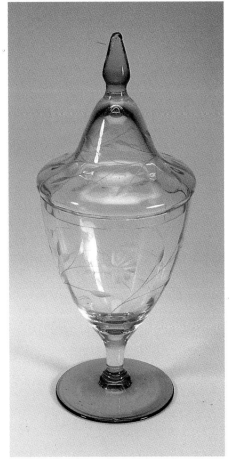

#14 1/2 Fairway 22 oz. Ritz Blue with Crystal knob and base candy jar with #2 cover. Circa 1930s 8.5" high. 4" in diameter. $350-395.

#1933 LMX (El Mexicano) cigarette box, two-piece with cover in Pink Quartz. 4 1/2" long x 3 1/2" wide. Circa 1930s. $225-250.

Compotes

Jellies are included here under compotes.

#7620 Rarey compote in Ritz Blue.with Crystal stem and foot. 6 1/2" high x 6" diameter. Circa 1930s. $225-250.

#7556 Toledo 4 1/2" compote with a #4 cover. Circa. 1920s. 8.75" high. $250-275.

#7643 Celeste low compote and cover. Ritz Blue with Crystal Golf Ball knob/ finial, stem and foot. Circa 1930s. 9" high, 6" in diameter. $350-395.

#7617 Ashford compote with Crystal stem and foot and Azure bowl. 5 3/4" high x 4 1/4" in diameter. Circa 1930s. $125-150.

#7654 Reverse Twist compote in Anna Rose with floral enamel decoration.
6 1/2" high x 6 3/4" in diameter. Circa 1930s. $150-165.

#7942 Lorain compote. Two-Tone Laurel color. Circa 1920s. 8 3/4" high x 5" in diameter. $125-140.

#7941 Ingrid covered compote, Crystal with #734 American Beauty etch.
6 1/2" high x 4 1/2" diameter. Circa 1930s. $200-225.

#7946 Carrick compote without a cover in Two-Tone Danube. Gold band and unknown cutting. 6" high x 4 1/2" in diameter. Circa 1930s. $150-175.

#7947 Mirmar compote. Two-Tone Danube with an unknown cutting. Circa 1920s. 6 1/4" high x 5" in diameter. $125-150.

#7946 Carrick fruit compote with light cutting. Two-Tone Laurel. Circa 1920s. 6" high x 4 1/2" in diameter. $125-150.

#7948 Palmer compote. Two-Tone Danube. Circa 1920s. 7 1/2" high x 5 1/4" in diameter. $125-150.

#7950 Melody jelly. Aquamarine. Circa 1928. 6 1/2" high. $150-175.

#7954 Brighton compote. Ritz Blue with Crystal stem and foot with a tear drop stem. Circa 1930s. 7" in diameter, 6" high. $225-250.

#7954 Brighton Old Bristol line compote. Ritz Blue with an Alabaster applied rim. Circa 1930s. 6" high, 6.75" in diameter. $450-500.

#7654 Reverse Twist compote in
Aquamarine. 6 1/4" high x 7" diameter.
Circa 1930s. $150-165.

#7956 Windsor compote with crimped
rim in the Old Bristol line. Circa 1930s.
7" high. 6" in diameter. $600-650.

Decanters, Servers, and Ice Buckets/Tubs

Decanters produced between 1899 and 1920 were usually Crystal. Many were decorated with nicely cut stoppers and necks. When these decanters were decorated, they generally featured either needle etchings or fairly simple glass cuttings (Wiley 1996, 2).

From 1921 to 1937, decanters were produced in a wider variety of shapes and featuring a more varied array of decorations. In 1921, for example, when the Two-Tone line was introduced, one of the most elegant forms in this line was the #24 Athens decanter in Danube (Wiley 1996, 4).

Among the more common decanter shapes produced during the Years of Elegance was the #10 1/2 Lynward. It has been found both decorated and undecorated in the rich, deep colors for which Morgantown's reputation was made. Other decanters of interest during this period were the #24 Circlet, the decanter with a tumbler stopper (in case a thirteenth thirsty soul shows up at the party or the owner is drinking alone) and the diminutive 16 oz. #29 Hartford, which was adorned with the Hollywood decoration (Wiley 1996, 3).

The Hollywood decoration itself was described as a combination of cool, satin frosting, featuring a glossy red band next to a wider Platinum band, accompanied by a transparent band in the upper area (*Turnover Topics* 1935, 8). This decoration was also made in black bands and green bands.

During the Guild years, there was a distinct lack of decanters. The #52 Tulsa was one interesting three-part decanter produced during the Decor years. It was made in several Decor colors but has been hard to find (Wiley 1996, 4).

In all, as of this writing, there are nineteen known decanter shapes and variations. Finding one of each could become a life-long challenge (Wiley 1996, 4).

#1 Little King decanter with Crystal octogan stopper in Ebony with Silver decoration. Shown with #9051 Zenith bar tumblers in Ebony with Silver bands. Decanter: 7" high, $400-450. Tumblers: 3" high, $50-60 each.

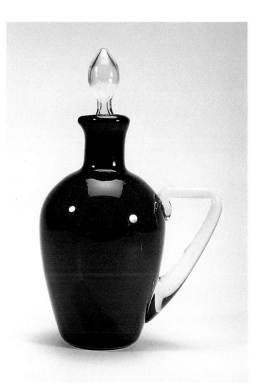

#2 Davis decanter (with a different stopper and a square handle) in Ritz Blue with a pulled lip and a Crystal handle and a Crystal stopper. 9 1/4" high. Circa 1930s. $350-400.

Zenith India Black bar tumbler with Platinum band. Decanter: $300-350; Tumbler: $40-45.

#2 Victory decanter with Crystal octagon stopper. Venetian Green with Peacock optic. 8" high. Circa 1930s. $275-325.

Left: #2 Victory decanters with octagon stoppers on a tantalis. Crystal with Silver lettering. 8 1/2" high. Circa 1930s. $500-550 set.

#10 1/2 Lynward decanter with Daisy stopper. Crystal with Platinum decoration. 11" high. #7630 Ballerina cordial with Platinum decoration. Circa 1931. 5" high x 1 1/2" in diameter. Decanter: $300-350; cordial: $35-40.

#10 1/2 Lynward decanter with Crystal sunflower stopper and green band Hollywood decoration (satin frosting on bottom with applied glossy green and band of bright Platinum on top.) Shown with a #7711 Callahan water with green band Hollywood decoration. Decanter: 11" high. Water: 7 1/2" high x 3 1/2" diameter. Circa 1930s. Decanter: $300-350; water: $40-45.

#10 1/2 Lynward decanter with a daisy stopper. Ritz Blue with a Platinum encrusted floral decoration. 11" high. Circa 1930s. $400-450.

#10 1/2 Lynward decanter with Daisy Crystal stopper. Stiegel Green with Platinum applied decoration. Circa 1930s. 11.5" high. $350-395.

Left: #10 1/2 Lynward decanter with a daisy stopper in Ebony with Platinum hunt scene decoration. 10 1/2" high. Circa 1930s. $400-450.

#10 1/2 Lynward decanter with an octagon Crystal stopper, Ritz Blue with a #769 Platinum Sparta etch with Platinum plain bands. 11.5" high decanter. $400-450. #8701 Garrett flat bottomed 9 oz. tumbler with #769 Platinum Sparta etch. $95-115. #9051 Zenith Ritz Blue bar 1 1/2 oz. tumbler, #769 Platinum Sparta etch. $95-115. Circa 1930s.

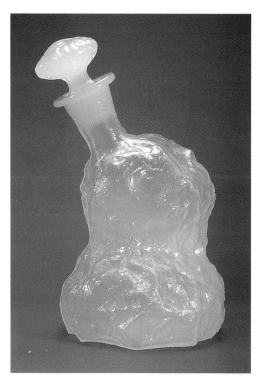

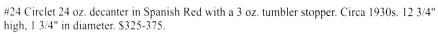

#24 Circlet 24 oz. decanter in Spanish Red with a 3 oz. tumbler stopper. Circa 1930s. 12 3/4" high, 1 3/4" in diameter. $325-375.

#1933 LMX (El Mexicano) decanter in Ice. 8" high. Circa 1930s. $200-225.

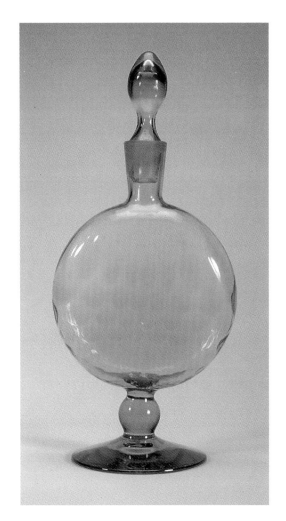

Left: #58 Canteen footed decanter with Peacock optic in Meadow Green. 10 1/2" high. Circa 1920s. $400-450.

#2124 Regina decanters with Crystal octogan stoppers in Stiegel Green in metal holder. 10" high. Circa 1930s. $600-650.

Cocktail Server

#1 Cadenza 24 oz. cocktail server. #749 Shamrock etch. Circa 1923. Removable top. 10" high. $190-210.

#7602 Gorman Jack Frost decor buckets. Left: Azure Blue satin finish. Right: Anna Rose satin finish. Both with icicles as part of the outside surface of body mold. 6" high x 4 3/4" diameter. Circa 1930s. $250-300.

Ice Buckets/Tubs

#1933 LMX ice tub in Ice. 4" high x 6" diameter. Circa 1930s. $150-175.

#9954 Karma 6" ice tub with Peacock optic in Gypsy Fire. Blown Crystal cover. Yes, this is a Guild period piece; however, it is the only ice tub from that period in the book so I chose to include it here with its predecessors. Circa 1960s. 6" high x 5 3/4" in diameter. $85-95.

Finger Bowls

#7639 finger bowl. Crystal with ebony foot. Faun etch. Circa 1930s. 4 1/8" in diameter. $100-125.

Jugs, Pitchers and Tankards

The #545 jug would be decorated with either the Sea Gulls or Hollywood decorative motif and was accompanied by the #9093 12 oz. tumblers. The Sea Gulls refreshment set had colors suggesting cool breezes of the sea and was described as ideal for summer. The Sea Gulls set retailed for five dollars (*Turnover Topics* 1935, 8).

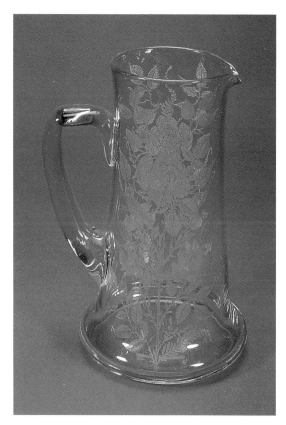

Crystal pitcher with #734 American Beauty etch. Flared base; handle flattened on top. 8" high. Circa 1930s. $250-295.

Unknown 54 oz. jug with #507 Iroquois cutting. Matching #8711 tumbler, 5 1/2 oz. Circa 1920s. Jug: 9 1/2" high. $250-275. Tumbler: 3 3/4" high x 2 1/2" in diameter. $25-30.

#2 Arcadia 54 oz. jug without cover. Crystal with a #734 American Beauty etch. Circa 1920s. 9 1/4" high. $275-295.

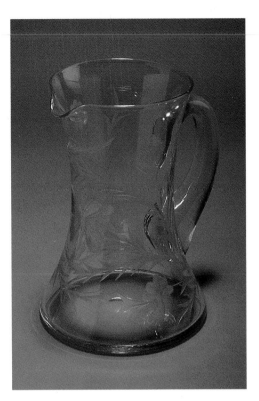

#2 Arcadia 54 oz. jug without cover. Crystal with a #734 American Beauty etch. 8 1/4" high. Circa 1930s. $295-325.

#8 Orleans 54 oz. jug. Crystal with butterfly and leaf cutting. Circa 1920. 8" high x 4 1/2" in diameter. $150-175.

#6 Kaufman 54 oz. tankard in Crystal with #734 American Beauty etch. 8 1/2" high. Circa 1930s. $250-295.

#10 1/2 Heacock 54 oz. jug. Crystal with floral cutting. Circa 1920s. 10 1/2" high. $225-250.

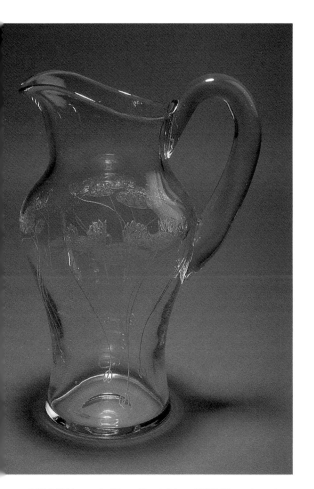

#22 Karma 54 oz. jug. Two-Tone Arctic (Crystal crackled jug and lid with Venetian Green handle and finial.) 9 1/2" high. $225-250.
Pair of # 8413 Oxford 12 oz. handled tumblers, Two Tone Arctic. Crystal crackled, Venetian Green handles.. 3 3/4" high x 2" in diameter. Circa mid-1920s. $25-30.

#10 1/2 Heacock 54 oz Crystal jug. #727 Victoria etch. Circa 1920. 10 1/2" high. $295-325.

#15 Saxony 54 oz. jug. Crystal with unknown blue and white enameling. Circa 1920. 9" high. $150-175.

#23 Karma 54oz Crystal jug with cover. #733 Virginia etch. Circa 1920. 7 1/4" high. $295-325.

#23 Karma 32 oz jug without cover. Crystal with #743 Bramble Rose etch. Circa 1920s. 7 1/4" high. $225-250.

#33 Rawsthorne 48 oz. jug Meadow Green, twisted reed handle, with Peacock optic. Circa 1930s. 7.5" high to lip. $250-275.

#31 Denten 30 oz. jug. Crystal with an unknown cutting. Circa 1920. 11 1/4" high. $225-250.

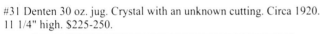

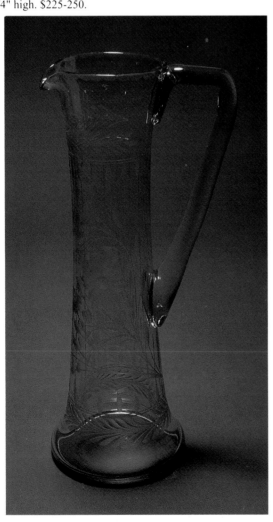

#34 Fontana 32 oz. footed jug. Two-Tone Genova. Circa 1920s. 11" high to lip. $375-425.

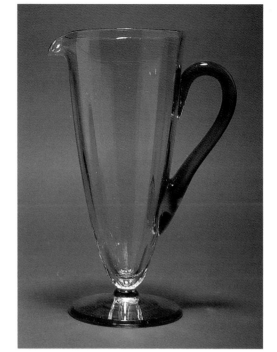

#34 Fontana 32 oz. footed jug. Two-Tone Laurel.Circa 1920s. 9" high. $300-350.

#34 Fontana 32 oz. footed jug. Two-Tone Danube. Lydia cutting. Circa 1921. 11 1/4" high at the lip. $400-425.

Believed to be a variation of #34 Fontana footed jug in Two-Tone Genova. 11 1/2" high to lip. Possibly an experimental lunchtime or after-hours piece. Circa 1920s. $375-425.

Right: #36 54 oz Bolero jug . Two-Tone Arctic. Crystal crackle with Venetian Green handle and foot. Circa 1920s. 10 1/2" high at highest point. $350-385.
Left: #9069 Hopper footed ice tea. Two-Tone Arctic. Crystal and Venetian Green. Circa 1920s. 5 1/2" high x 2 3/4" in diameter. $35-40.

#36 Bolero 54 oz. jug. Two-Tone Danube with unknown cutting. Circa 1920s. 10" high. $350-375.

#36 Bolero 54 oz. jug. Two-Tone Danube. Lydia cutting. Circa 1921. 11" high at the lip. $350-375.

#37 Barry 48 oz. jug. Two-Tone Arctic color. Crystal with Venetian handle and foot. 9 1/4" high x 6" in diameter. Circa 1930s. $300-350.

#37 Barry 48 oz. jug in Two-Tone Laurel with a Lotus etch. Circa 1930s. 8 1/2" high. $325-375.

#37 Barry 48 oz. crackle jug with matte finish and nasturtium flower decoration and Gold band. 9" high. Circa 1930s. $450-495.

#37 Barry 48 oz. jug. Venetian Green bowl with Jade handle and foot. 9" high x 6 1/4" in diameter. Circa 1930s. $400-450.

Left: #37 Barry 48 oz. jug with #758 Sunrise Medallion etch. Azure blue. Circa 1930s. 9" high x 6 1/4" in diameter. $500-550.

Bottom left: #37 Barry 48 oz. jug. Crystal with an Ebony foot and handle with #777 Baden etch. 9 1/4" high x 6 1/4" in diameter. Circa 1930s. $425-475.

Below: #37 Barry 48 oz. jug. Crystal bowl, Ebony handle and foot. #781 Fontinelle etch. Circa 1931. 9 1/4" high x 6" in diameter. $500-550.

#37 Barry 48 oz jug. Crystal with #784 Carleton "Marco" etch. Platinum encrusted #31 band. Circa 1931. 9 1/2" high x 6 1/2" in diameter. $395-425.

#42 1/2 O'Kane 54 oz. jug in Meadow Green with a cover and a Palm optic. Circa 1920s. 7 1/2" high to lip. $325-375.

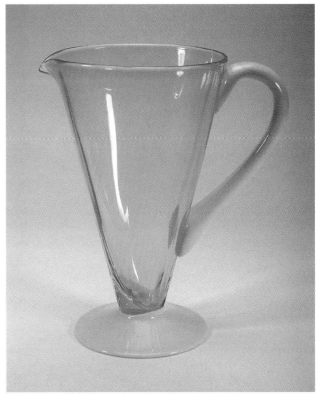

#37 Barry 48oz. jug. Spanish Red with Venetia painted Gold decoration, combines the #808 Mikado etch with the #29 border. 8 1/2" high to lip. $500-550.

#48 Vanessa 48 oz. jug. Meadow Green with Alabaster handle and foot. 9 1/2" high x 6" in diameter. Circa 1930s. $450-500.

#49 Jubilee 28 oz. jug. Ritz Blue with Crystal handle and base. 7" high to lip. $250-300.

#48 Vanessa 54 oz. Crystal jug with unknown cutting. Circa 1930s. 9 1/2" high x 6 1/2" in diameter at top. $325-370.

#49 Jubilee 54 oz. jug. Ritz Blue with Crystal handle and base. Circa 1930s. 7 1/2" high to lip. $320-350.

#48 Vanessa 54oz. jug. Crystal with ebony foot and handle and #768 LeMons etch. 9 1/2" high x 6" in diameter. $550-600.

#49 54 oz. Stiegel Green jug with applied square Crystal foot and Crystal handle. Circa 1930s. 8.5" high to lip. $350-395.

#545 Pickford 54 oz. jug. Crystal with Jade handle and #345 1/2 White Gold needle etch and Platinum band. Repaired lip. 8 1/2" high. Circa 1930s. $375-425.

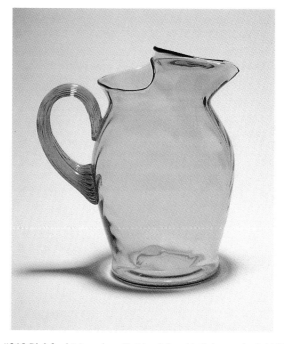

#545 Pickford 54 oz. jug. Golden Iris with Palm optic. 8 1/4" high to lip. Circa 1930s. $325-365.

#544 Sandra 70 oz. jug. Crystal Craquelle (crackled glass) with Nanking Blue handle. Circa 1930s. 8" high. $395-425.

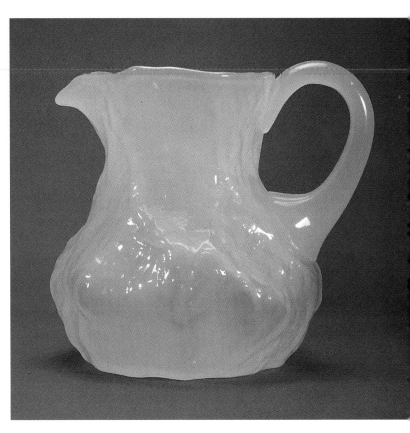

#545 Pickford 54 oz. jug. Meadow Green with Palm optic and reed handle. 8" high to lip. $325-365.

#1933 Del Rey LMX (El Mexicano) jug in Ice. 6 1/2" high. Circa 1930s. $200 235.

#546 Roulette 54 oz. jug in Stiegel Green with Crystal handle. 8" high. Circa 1930s. $650-750.

#1933 LMX Ockner jug in Pink Quartz. 7" high. Circa 1930s. $250-300.

#7622 1/2 Ringling 54 oz. jug. Ritz Blue with Crystal handle and enameled white rings. 8 1/2" high to the lip. 1935. $250-295.

#1933 LMX Ockner 50 oz. jug in Seaweed with matching #802 tumbler. Circa 1930s. Jug: 7 1/2" high x 5" in diameter. $150-175. Tumbler: 4" high x 3" in diameter. $25-30.

#20069 Melon 54 oz. jug. Alabaster with Ritz Blue handle, shown with a #20069 Melon 12 oz. tumbler. Alabaster with Ritz Blue foot. Circa 1931. Jug: 9" high. $700-800. Tumbler: 6" high x 3 1/2" in diameter. $125-150.

#20069 Melon 54 oz. jug. Crystal with matte finish and Ebony handle; Aurora etch. 9" high. Circa 1930s. $1500-1800.

Marmalade Jars with Covers

#107 Dubarry marmalade with cover. Crystal with #727 Victoria etch. 4" high. Circa pre-1920s. $175-200.

#9074 Belton marmalade. Crystal with Gold decoration on lid and bowl, Gold band on knob and foot. 7" high, including lid. Circa 1920s. $125-150.

Muddlers

Muddlers were introduced to the wholesale trade in the March 1935 issue of the *Old Morgantown Turnover Topics*. Of the two, the ball muddlers are fairly common while the spoon muddlers are quite difficult to come by. Both of the muddlers shown here have reeded handles and Ritz Blue cased filaments. Muddlers have also been found with other cased filament colors (Wiley 1997, 2).

But ... what the devil is a *muddler*? In 1935, the Turnover Topics solved this particular mystery for all the tea totallers out there. The muddler was for cocktails. The spoon muddler was described as having a dual purpose, the straight end (or muddler) was a drink stirrer and the other end was a spoon. "Combination spoon-muddlers have only recently been offered by Old Morgantown. Of the samples shown here, five have 'cased' colors in the handles that diffuse over the somewhat wider area in the bowl of the spoon. ... The dual purpose and the cased colors make these particularly ingenious and more than double their attractiveness to those who like to serve a dash of beauty with their old fashioned cocktails." These were listed as available in the following colors: Crystal-Blue, Amberola, Crystal-Green, and all-Crystal. The spoon muddlers shown in the 1935 advertisement were offered six to a card at a retail price of $1.75 and $2.00 per card, depend-

ing on the colors. A sample card containing five cased and one all-Crystal muddler would be sent post-paid for one dollar to any dealer who preferred to look before buying (*Turnover Topics* 1935, 9).

Novelty muddlers in Crystal with Ritz Blue filament. Circa 1930s. Left: with spoon bowl, 4.75" long. $65-75; right: with a ball, 5" long. $55-65.

Napkin Rings

#1 Napkin Ring. Crystal with #1 Marielle cutting. 1" high x 1 1/2" in diameter. $50-60.

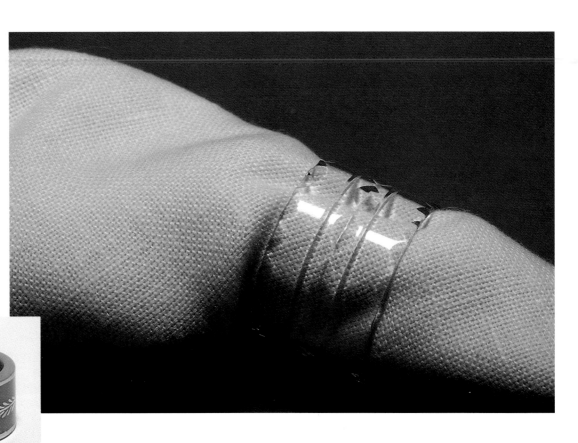

#1 Napkin ring in Jade Green with Gold applied decoration. Circa 1930s. 1" high, 1 1/2" in diameter. $75-85.

Night Sets and Guest Sets

Night Sets

Left and above: #24 Maria 4 piece night or medicine set in Azure with unknown floral cutting and Panel optic. 7" high. Circa 1930s. $450-500.

Left and below: #24 Maria 3-piece night or medicine set in Azure Blue with Peacock optic and painted floral decoration. 6 3/4" high. Circa 1930s. $250-300 (This price reflects the fact that the tumbler is missing.)

Guest Sets

Above and right: #23 Margaret guest set in Anna Rose with unknown cutting. 6 1/4" high. Circa 1930s. $300-350.

#23 Margaret Jade guest set with painted (unfired) floral decoration. Circa 1920s. 6" high. $175-195.

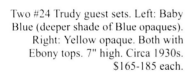

Two #24 Trudy guest sets. Left: Baby Blue (deeper shade of Blue opaques). Right: Yellow opaque. Both with Ebony tops. 7" high. Circa 1930s. $165-185 each.

#24 Trudy guest set in Jade Green with peacock and floral decoration. 6 1/4" high. Circa 1930s. $175-200 with this decoration.

Toilet Sets

Toilet bottle set. Alabaster decorated. Lotion bottle has Swan decoration; toilet water bottle has Dresden decoration. Both are 4" high to the top of the lid. $50-60 each.

Plates, Cups and Saucers

Plates

Included under plates are a relish dish and a saucer.

8" Crystal plate with #796 Floret etch. Circa 1930s. $15-18.

8 1/2" Crystal plate with variation of #796 Floret etch (compare to plate in previous photograph). Circa 1930s. $15-18.

#1511 round plate, Crystal with unknown cutting. Circa 1930s. 7 1/2" in diameter. $18-20.

#1511 round plate, Crystal with Picardy etch. Circa 1930s. 8" in diameter. $15-18.

#1511 round plate, Crystal with #734 American Beauty etch . Circa 1930s. 7 1/2" in diameter. $20-23.

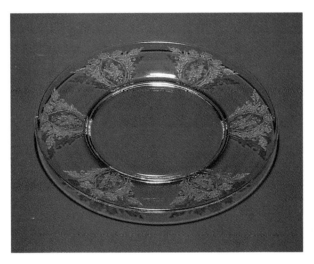

#1511 round plate, Crystal with Saranac etch. Circa 1930s. 7 1/2" in diameter. $18-20.

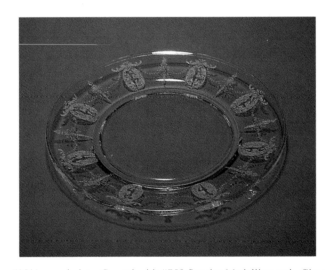

#1511 round plate, Crystal with #758 Sunrise Medallion etch. Circa 1930s. 7 1/2" in diameter. $25-30.

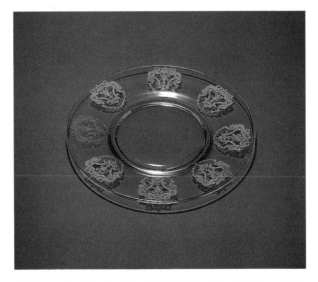

#1511 round plate, Crystal with #733 Virginia etch. Circa 1930s. 7 1/2" in diameter. $15-18.

#1511 round plate, Crystal with # 765 Springtime etch . Circa 1930s. 7 1/2" in diameter. $15-18.

#1511 round plate, Crystal with #777 Baden etch. Circa 1930s. 7 1/2" in diameter. $20-23.

#1511 round plate, Anna Rose with Palm optic. Circa 1930s. 7 1/2" diameter. $15-18.

#1511 round plate, Crystal with #778 Carlton etch. Circa 1930s. 7 1/2" in diameter. $15-18.

#1511 round plate, Anna Rose with #758 Sunrise Medallion etch. Circa 1930s. 7 1/2" diameter. $30-35.

#1511 round plate, Crystal with #795 Versailles etch. Circa 1930s. 7 1/2" in diameter. $15-18.

#1511 round plate, Azure Blue with #756 Tinkerbell etch. Circa 1930s. 7 1/2" in diameter. $35-40.

#1511 round plate, Azure Blue with #758 Sunrise Medallion etch. Circa 1930s. 7 1/2" in diameter. $30-35.

#1520 square saucer , Ebony, 5 1/2". Circa 1930s. $10-12.

#1511 round plate, Meadow Green with #751 Adonis etch. Circa 1930s. 7.5" in diameter. $30-35.

#1933 LMX (El Mexicano) relish in Ice. 8" wide x 9" long. Circa 1930s. $100-125.

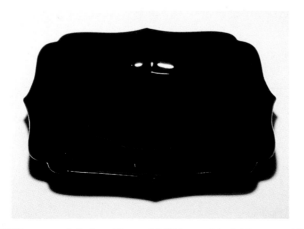

#1519 square salad plate, Ebony, 8 1/2" (part of the bridge ensemble shown in the 1931 catalog). Circa 1930s. $15-17.

Salt and Pepper Shakers

#2 Federal 2 7/8" individual salt dip. Crystal with India black stem. Circa 1930s. $20-25.

#4 Regal salt and pepper shakers in Ritz Blue. 4 1/2" high. Circa 1930s. $250-300 pair.

#3 Goodman salt and pepper shakers, Ritz Blue, Crystal feet. 4" high. Circa 1930s. $250-300 pair.

#5 Henderson salt and pepper shakers in Spanish Red. 4 5/8" high. Circa 1930s. $250-300 pair.

#6 Bowman salt and pepper shakers . Jade and Jade with Ebony band decorations. 2 1/4" high. Circa 1930s. Jade shakers: $85-110 pair; Jade with Ebony shakers: $110-125 pair.

#6 Bowman salt and pepper shakers in Ritz Blue with Platinum band decoration. 2 1/4" high. Circa 1920s. $125-150 pair.

Stemwares

Some footed tumblers are included in this section for comparative purposes. One of the most recognizable stems from the pre-Guild years is the Golf Ball. While the average stem required a "shop" of four workers to complete, the labor-intensive Golf Ball stem required a shop of sixteen men to finish.

One of the most elegant and fragile of the Morgantown stems is the rare stem commonly referred to as the "Square." This stem with the open square in its upper half is believed to have been introduced in 1929, during a period described by Leora Leasure as a, "... time when elegance was defined as fine dining (Leasure 1996, 4)."

One example of the Square stem is the #7637 Courtney, which has been seen with a frosted stem and crystal bowl.

5 1/2 oz. champagne. Ebony cased filament stem. #747 Baden etch. 4 3/4" high x 4" in diameter. $95-110.

Compare the simple shape of this goblet used in the early Guild period as institutional glassware with its more elegant predecessors. #7011 Hartley 10 oz. goblet in Ritz Blue with Crystal foot. 5 1/4" high x 3" diameter. Circa late 1930s. $30-35.

#7577 Venus 9 oz. Crystal goblet. Needle etch #207. 4 3/4" high x 2" in diameter. $18-20.

#7113 Florida 9 oz. Crystal goblet. #796 Floret etch with Meadow Green foot. Circa 1923. 5 1/2" high x 3 1/2" in diameter. $40-50.

#7585 1/2 Cotillion 12 oz. ice tea and 9 oz. luncheon goblet, Crystal bowl with Palm optic with Anna Rose foot and stem. Ice tea: 7" high x 4" in diameter. Goblet: 5" high x 3 1/4" in diameter. Circa 1930s. Ice tea: $45-50; luncheon goblet: $40-45.

Left: #7587 Hanover Crystal champagne. #743 Bramble
Rose etch. Circa 1918. 5" high x 3 1/4" in diameter. $18-22.
Right: #7587 Hanover parfait. #743 Bramble Rose etch.
Circa 1918. 5 1/2" high x 2" in diameter. $22-26.

#7604 1/2 Heirloom 9 oz. goblet.
Crystal with an unknown needle
etch with Platinum band. 8 1/4"
high x 4 3/4" in diameter. Circa
1931. $32-36.

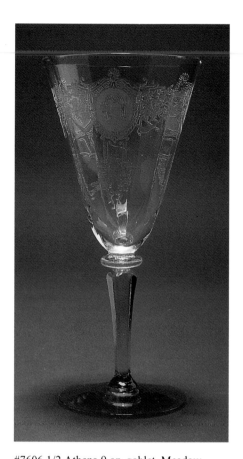

#7606 1/2 Athena 9 oz. goblet. Meadow
Green stem and foot. #751 Adonis etch. Circa
1931. 7 1/2" high x 3 1/2" in diameter.
$80-90.

#7606 1/2 Athena 9 oz. goblet. Ebony
cased filament stem. #776 Nasreen
etch. 7 1/2" high x 3 3/4" in diameter.
Circa 1931. $85-95.

#7604 1/2 Heirloom 9 oz. goblet.
14K Topaz, #751 Adonis etch. Circa
1931. 8" high x 3 3/4" in diameter.
$50-60.

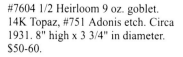

#7606 1/2 Athena 9 oz. goblet. Crystal bowl and foot; Ebony cased filament stem. #778 Carlton etch. Circa 1931. 7 1/2" high x 3 3/4" in diameter. $85-95.

#7606 1/2 Athena 5 1/2 oz. sherbet. Crystal bowl, Ebony cased filament stem, with a #776 Nasreen etch. Circa 1931. 3 3/4" high x 3 3/4" in diameter. $60-70.

#7606 1/2 Athena cafe parfait. Crystal with Ebony cased filament stem. #778 Carlton etch. 6" high. Circa 1930s. $125-150.

#7606 1/2 Athena wine. Ebony cut cased filament stem. Unknown cutting. Circa 1930s. 6" high x 2 1/2" in diameter. $65-75.

#7606 1/2 Athena 3 1/2 oz. cocktail. Crystal bowl and foot; Ebony cased filament stem. #778 Carlton etch. Circa 1931. 5" high x 3 3/4" in diameter. $65-75.

#7616 1/2 Wescott
cordial. Crystal bowl with
Spanish Red cased
filament stem. Circa
1930s. 4" high, 1 1/4" in
diameter. $70-80.

Left and above: #7617 Brilliant 10 oz.
goblet with Golden Iris stem and foot
decorated with Gold Rosamond etch
and Gold band. 7 1/4" high by 3 1/4"
diameter. Circa 1920s. $150-175.

Assortment of #7620 Fontanne with #781 Fontinelle etch and Ebony cased filament
stem. Back row, left to right: 4 1/2 oz. cafe parfait, 6 3/4" high $160-175; 9 oz. goblet,
7 3/4" x 3 1/2" in diameter, $160-175; 6 oz. saucer champagne, 6 1/4" high x 4" in
diameter, $125-150. Front row, left to right: 3 1/2oz. cocktail, 5 1/4" high x 3" in
diameter, $110-125; 6 oz. sherbet, 4 1/4" high x 3 3/4" in diameter, $110-125; 3 oz.
wine, 6" high x 2 1/4" in diameter, $125-150.

Selection of #7620 1/2 Fontainebleau, Crystal bowls with Meadow Green stems and feet, and Floradora etch. Back left: goblet, 7 1/4" high. Back right: parfait, 6 1/4" high. Front: cocktail, 5 1/2" high. Circa 1930s. Goblet: $65-75; parfait: $75-85; cocktail: $50-55.

#7620 Fontanne 9 oz goblet. Meadow Green bowl, Crystal stem and foot. #781 Fontinelle etch. Circa 1931. 7 1/2" high x 3 1/2" in diameter. $175-195.

#7623 Crystal satinized Pygon wine. Bird decoration by Dorothy Thorpe. 5 3/4" high x 2 1/8" diameter. Circa 1930s. $175-200.

#7620 Fontanne cocktail in Anna Rose with Crystal Stem and Foot. #781 Fontinelle etch. 5 1/2" x 3" in diameter. Circa 1930s. $150-175.

#7624 Paragon 10 oz. goblet. Crystal with Gold decoration. Gold stem. Circa 1929. 8 1/4" high x 3 1/2" in diameter. $95-110.

#7624 Paragon 5 1/2 oz. champagne. Crystal. Unknown cutting. Circa 1929. 6" high x 4" in diameter. $75-85.

#7625 Parma luncheon goblet. Crystal bowl and foot with Alabaster stem. #758 Sunrise Medallion etch. 6" high x 3" diameter. Circa 1930s. $160-175.

#7630 Ballerina 9 oz. goblet. Azure Blue with #758 Sunrise Medallion etch. Circa 1931. 8" high x 3 1/4" in diameter. $75-85.

#7630 Ballerina cafe parfait in Azure Blue with #758 Sunrise Medallion etch. Circa 1930s. 6 1/2" high x 2 1/4" in diameter. $100-125.

#7631 Jewel 9 oz. goblet. Azure Blue with #756 Tinkerbell etch. Circa 1927. 7 1/2" high x 2 3/4" in diameter. $125-140.

#7631 Jewel 9 oz. goblet. Meadow Green stem and foot. Unknown cutting. Circa 1927. 7 1/4" high x 3 1/4" in diameter. $60-68.

#7634 Tiburon 9 oz. goblet. Venetian Green stem and foot. #760 Kyoto etch. 7 3/4" high x 3 1/4" in diameter. $70-80.

#7634 Tiburon 9 oz. goblet. Ebony cased filament stem. #777 Baden etch. 7 1/2" high x 3 1/4" in diameter. Circa 1931. $75-85.

#7631 Jewel sherbet in Azure Blue with #756 Tinkerbell etch. Circa 1927. 4 1/2" high x 3 1/2" in diameter. $95-110.

#7634 Tiburon 6 oz. champagne. Ebony cased filament stem. #747 Baden etch. 6" high x 4 1/2" in diameter. $75-85.

#7634 Tiburon 2 1/2 oz. wine; Rainbow (iridized) bowl with Azure Blue foot and stem. Circa 1930s. 5 3/4" high x 2" in diameter. $40-45.

#7636 Square 5 1/2 oz. champagne. Crystal. 6 3/4" high x 4" in diameter. Circa 1929. $135-150.

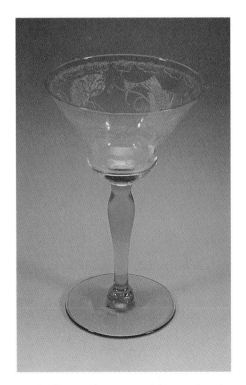

#7635 Oceana champagne with Aquaria etch. Venetian Green stem and foot with Crystal bowl. 6" high x 3 3/4" in diameter. Circa 1930s. $140-160.

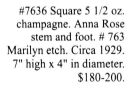

#7636 Square 5 1/2 oz. champagne. Anna Rose stem and foot. # 763 Marilyn etch. Circa 1929. 7" high x 4" in diameter. $180-200.

#7637 Courtney 4 1/2 oz. claret with a
Dorothy C. Thorpe decorated satin stem.
Crystal. Circa 1929. 7" high x 2 3/4" in
diameter. $175-190.

Below: Grouping of three #7640 Art
Moderne 9 oz. goblets showing various
etch decorations. $125-150 each.

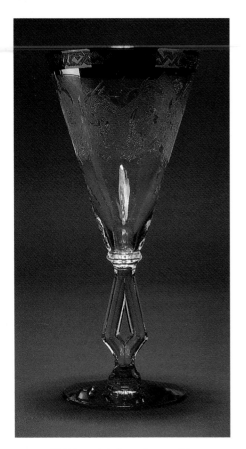

#7640 Art Moderne 9 oz. goblet. Platinum #3 band and Labelle etch. All Crystal. 7 1/2" high x 3 1/2" in diameter. $125-145.

#7640 Art Moderne 9 oz. goblet in Ritz Blue with Crystal stem and foot. Gold encrusted #768 LeMons decoration. 7 1/2" high x 3 1/2" diameter. Circa 1930s. $150-175.

#7640 Art Moderne 5 1/2 oz. champagne. Faun etch. Cryatal bowl and foot; Ebony stem. Circa 1931. 5 1/2" high x 4 1/4" in diameter. $115-125.

#7640 Art Moderne cordial. Crystal bowl with Ebony stem. #768 Le Mons etch and Gold trim on bowl and foot. Circa 1930s. 5" high x 1 3/4" in diameter. $150-175.

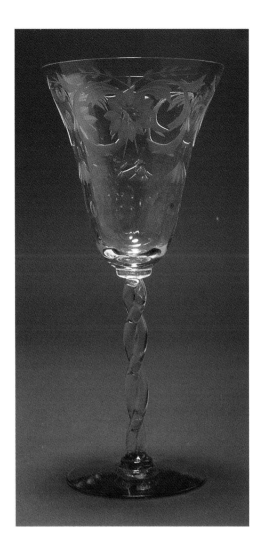

#7643 Golf Ball 21 oz. brandy snifter. Spanish Red with Crystal stem/foot. Circa 1930s. 6 1/4" high, 3" in diameter. $150-175.

Left: #7642 Princess 9 oz, goblet. Crystal with Venetian Green stem and foot. Flirtation cutting. 8 1/2" high x 3 3/4" in diameter. $70-80.

Selection of #7643 Golf Ball line. Back row, from left: goblet in Spanish Red with Crystal stem and foot, $50-55; sherbet in Ritz Blue, $35-40; champagne in Spanish Red, $35-40; cocktail in Stiegel Green, $30-35; claret in Stiegel Green, $50-60; wine in Ritz Blue, $35-40; cordial in Spanish Red, $50-55.

#7643 Golf Ball line in White. Back left: Water, 6 3/4" high x 3 1/4" diameter. Back right: champagne, 5" high x 3 1/2" diameter. Front: cocktail, 4" high x 3" diameter. Water: $95-110; champagne: $75-85; cocktail: $65-75.

#7643 Golf Ball in Ritz Blue with Crystal stem and foot; #769 Sparta etch. Left: champagne, 5" high x 3 1/2" diameter. Right: 9 oz. goblet, 6 1/2" high x 3 1/4" diameter. Circa 1930s. $85-95 each.

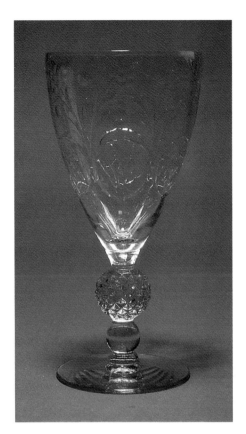

#7643 Golf Ball 9 oz. Crystal goblet with unknown cutting. Circa 1930s. 7" high x 3 1/4" in diameter. $40-45.

#7643 Golf Ball 9 oz. goblet. Flower and leaf design cutting. 6 1/2" high x 3 1/4" in diameter. $45-50.

#7643 Golf Ball 9 oz. goblet. Ritz Blue with Crystal stem and foot and a #769 Gold Sparta etch. Circa 1930s. 6 3/4" high, 3 1/4" in diameter. $100-125.

#7643 Golf Ball 9 oz. Crystal goblet with deep cutting. Circa 1930s. 7" high x 3 1/4" in diameter. $40-45.

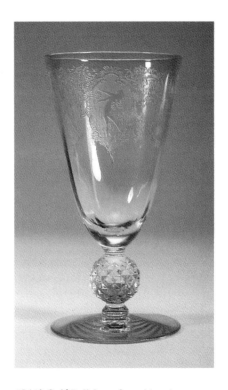

#7643 Golf Ball 9 oz. footed luncheon goblet. 14K Topaz with #781 Fontinelle etch. Crystal stem and foot. Circa 1930s. 6" high x 3 1/4" in diameter. $175-195.

#7643 Golf Ball Irish coffee in Ritz Blue with Crystal stem and foot. 4 3/4" high x 2 1/2" diameter. Circa 1930s. $150-175.

#7643 Golf Ball 3 oz. wine in Ritz Blue with Crystal foot and stem; #769 Sparta decoration. 4 1/2" high x 2" diameter. Circa 1930s. $80-90.

#7646 Sophisticate 9 oz. goblet with Picardy etch. Circa 1920s. 7" high x 4" in diameter. $25-30.

7643 Golf Ball 5 1/2 oz. champagne. Crystal with light floral cutting Circa 1930s. 5" high x 3 1/2" in diameter. $30-34.

#7643 Golf Ball 1 1/2 oz. Cordial, Crystal with cut decoration. 3 1/2" high x 1 1/2" in diameter. $45-50.

Right: #7653 Cantata 9 oz. goblet with #784 Carleton "Marco" decoration. #31 Platinum encrusted border. Circa 1931. 8" high x 3 1/2" in diameter. $75-85.

#7653 Cantata goblet in Anna Rose with a #777 Baden Etch. 8" high, 3 1/2" in diameter. Circa 1930. $65-75.

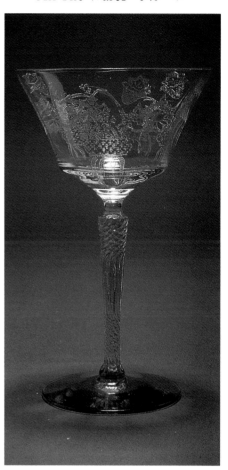

#7654 Lorna champagne. Venetian Green stem and foot. #766 Nantucket etch. Circa 1931. 6 1/2" high x 3 3/4" in diameter. $80-90.

#7654 Lorna 9 oz. goblet. Crystal with Lotus etch. Circa 1930s. 8   1/4" high x 3 1/4" in diameter. $50-60.

#7654 H.I.O. 3 1/2 oz. cocktail in Spanish Red with hunt scene Silver decoration by Lotus. 5 1/2" high. $150-175.

#7654 1/2 Legacy 10 oz. goblet with Superba etch and Ebony stem. Circa 1931. 8" high x 3 1/2" in diameter. $195-225.

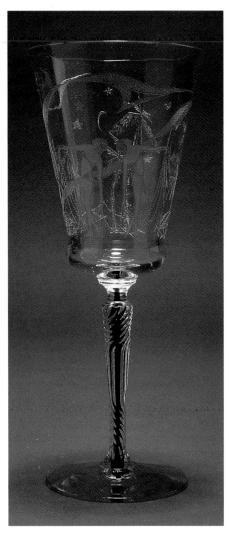

#7654 1/2 Legacy champagne with a Meadow Green foot and stem with Superba etch. 6 1/2" high x 4" in diameter. Circa 1930s. $165-185.

#7654 1/2 Legacy 9 oz. Crystal goblet. Has an Ebony cased filament stem. Superba etch. 8" high x 3 1/2" in diameter. Circa 1931. $175-195.

Left: #7654 1/2 Legacy 3 oz. cocktail, Crystal. Superba etch. 5" high x 3" in diameter. Circa 1931. $60-70.
Right: #7654 1/2 Legacy 5 1/2 oz. saucer champagne, Crystal. Superba etch. Meadow Green foot and stem. 6 1/2" high x 4" in diameter. Circa 1931. $165-185.

#7660 Empire 10 oz. Crystal goblet
with unknown cutting. Circa 1931.
7 1/4" high x 4" in diameter.
$35-40.

#7654 1/2 Legacy 3 oz. Crystal cocktail with an
Ebony stem. Superba etch. 5" high x 3" in
diameter. Circa 1931. $125-150.

#7659 1/2 Lenox 3 1/2 oz. cocktail.
Crystal bowl and foot with Spanish Red
cased filament stem. 6 1/4" high x 3"
diameter. Circa 1930s. $45-50.

Left: #7656 Astrid 9 oz. goblet. Anna
Rose color. #734 American Beauty
etch. 7 1/2" high x 3 1/4" in diameter.
$75-85.

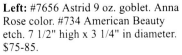

#7660 Empire water goblet, Crystal with
unknown etch. 7 1/4" high x 4" diameter.
Circa 1930s. $65-75.

#7660 1/2 Empress 10 oz. goblet. Spanish Red bowl with Crystal foot. Circa 1931. 7 1/4" high, 4" in diameter. $50-55.

Selection of #7664 Queen Anne stemware in Crystal and Azure Blue with assorted etchs. Back row, from left: water goblet, 8 1/2" high x 3 1/2" diameter, $100-125; tall chamagne, 8" high x 4" diameter, $175-195; medium champagne, 6 3/4" high x 3 3/4" diameter, $85-95; short champagne, 5 1/4" high x 4" diameter, $75-85. Front row, from left: parfait, 7 1/2" high x 2 1/4" diameter, $125-150; cocktail, 5 1/2" high x 3" diameter, $65-75; cordial, 5" high x 2 3/4" diameter, $175-200. All circa 1930s.

#7664 Queen Anne 10 oz. goblet. Crystal with unknown cutting. Circa 1931. 8 1/2" high x 3 1/2" in diameter. $65-75.

#7660 1/2 Empress parfait with a Spanish Red bowl and a Crystal stem and foot. 6 3/4" high x 2 3/4" in diameter. Circa 1930s. $70-80.

Right: #7664 Queen Anne 10 oz. goblet. Crystal with #757 Elizabeth etch. Circa 1931. 8 1/2" high x 3 1/4" in diameter. $75-85.

#7664 Queen Anne parfait. Anna Rose color. #758 Sunrise Medallion etch. 7 1/4" high x 2 1/4" in diameter. Circa 1931. $125-140.

#7664 Queen Anne 10 oz. goblet. Anna Rose. #758 Sunrise Medallion etch. Circa 1931. 8 1/2" high x 3 1/4" in diameter. $95-110.

#7664 Queen Anne 10 oz. goblet with Duo-tone Manchester Pheasant silkscreen design. Circa 1931. 8 1/2" high x 3 1/4" in diameter. $175-195.

Left: #7664 Queen Anne 10 oz. goblet. Azure Blue with a Woodland etch. Circa 1931. 8 1/2" high x 3 1/4" in diameter. $75-85.

#7664 Queen Anne 6 1/2 oz. champagne. Crystal with a Superba etch. Circa 1931. 8" high x 4" in diameter. $175-195.

#7664 Queen Anne 2 3/4 oz. cocktail. Crystal with unknown cutting. Circa 1930s. 5 1/2" high x 3" in diameter. $40-50.

#7665 Laura 9 oz. goblet. 14K Topaz bowl with Crystal stem and foot. #778 Carlton Madrid etch. 8 1/4" high x 3 1/2" in diameter. Circa 1931. $75-85.

#7669 Grandeur luncheon goblet with and #734 American Beauty etch. 6 3/4" high x 4 3/4" diameter. Circa 1930s. $40-45.

Left: #7665 Laura champagne in 14K Topaz with #776 Nasreen etch. 6" high x 4 1/4" diameter. **Right:** #7665 Laura flared oyster cocktail in 14K Topaz with #776 Nasreen etch. 3" high x 3" diameter. Circa 1930s. Champagne: $60-70; oyster cocktail: $50-60.

#7673 Lexington footed goblet. Ritz Blue cased filament stem. #790 Fairwin etch. 6 1/4" high x 3 1/4" in diameter. Circa 1931. $95-110.

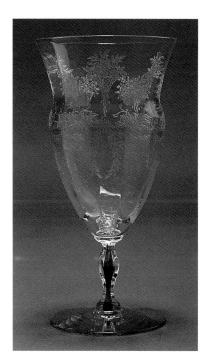

#7675 Paula 10 oz. goblet. Ritz Blue cased filament stem. Crystal bowl and foot. #787 Maytime etch. Circa 1931. 6 3/4" high x 3 1/2" in diameter. $85-95.

#7673 Lexington goblet with #798 Eileen etch and Gold band. 7 1/2" high x 2 3/4" diameter. Circa 1930s. $75-85.

#7673 Lexington 5 1/2 oz. saucer champagne. Ritz Blue cased filament stem. #790 Fairwin etch. 6 1/2" high x 4" in diameter. Circa 1931. $90-100.

#7675 Paula 5 1/2 oz. champagne. Ritz Blue cased filament stem. Crystal bowl and foot. #787 Maytime etch. Circa 1931. 6 1/2" high x 4" in diameter. $85-95.

Selection of #7678 Old English line. Back row, from left: goblet in Stiegel Green, $50-60; champagne in Stiegel Green, $40-45; sherbet in Spanish Red, $40-45. Front row, from left: claret in Ritz Blue, $50-60; cocktail in Spanish Red, $35-40; cordial/sherry in Ritz Blue, $50-60.

Compare the stemware above to the selection of #7678 Old English: ice tea in Spanish Red; luncheon in Ritz Blue; juice in Stiegel Green. All with Crystal stem and foot. Ice tea and luncheon: $45-50; juice: $40-45.

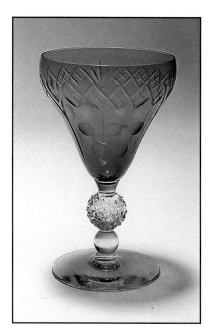

#7678 Old English goblet with Stiegel Green bowl, Crystal stem and foot. Unknown cutting. Circa 1930s. 6 1/4" high x 3 3/4" in diameter. $65-75.

#7682 Ramona 11 oz. goblet in Stiegel Green with Crystal stem and foot. 6 1/2" high x 3 1/2" diameter. Circa 1930s. $50-60.

Left: #7682 Ramona cordial in Ritz Blue with Crystal stem and foot. 3 3/4" high x 2" diameter. Right: #7682 Ramona cocktail in Ritz Blue with Crystal stem and foot. 4" high x 2 1/4" diameter. Circa 1930s. Cordial: $85-95; cocktail: $30-35.

#7683 Inwood champagne with Palm optic. Crystal bowl and Anna Rose stem and foot. 5 3/4" high x 3 3/4" in diameter. Circa 1930s. $35-40.

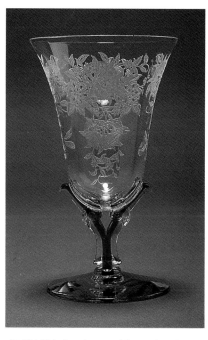

#7684 Yale luncheon goblet. #796 Floret etch. Ritz Blue cased filament stem. Circa 1932. 6" high x 3 1/2" in diameter. $175-195.

#7685 Radiant stem champagne on a Crystal square foot in Spanish Red. 4 3/4" high x 4" wide. Circa 1935. $50-60.

Selection of barware with #7688 1/2
Roanoke stem. Left: parfait in Fire and
Ice. 6 1/2" high. Right: cocktail,
Crystal bowl with amber stem and
foot, Cascade optic. 5" high. Parfait:
$50-60; cocktail: $40-45.

#7688 Jamestown drambuie.
Crystal with Ruby foot.
5 1/2" high. Circa 1930s.
$50-60.

#7689 Fairfax 9 oz. goblet. Unknown
cutting. 6 1/2" high x 3 1/4" in diameter.
$35-39.

#7688 1/2 Roanoke champagne.
Crystal with unknown cutting. Circa
1930s. 5" high x 4" in diameter. $30-
35.

#7688 1/2 Roanoke 9 oz. Crystal goblet
with unknown cutting. Circa 1930s.
6 1/4" high x 3 3/4" in diameter.
$35-40.

#7690 Monroe 9 oz. goblet with Saranac
etch. Circa 1932. 8 1/2" high x 3 3/4" in
diameter. $50-55.

Selection of #7690 Monroe stemware including a goblet, champagne, wine, cocktail, cordial, and three footed tumblers, Spanish Red bowls with Crystal stems and feet. Back row, from left: 9 oz. goblet, 8 1/4" high x 3 3/4" diameter, $60-70; champagne. 6 1/4" high x 4 1/4" diameter, $45-50; wine, 6" high x 2 1/2" diameter, $45-55; cocktail, 5 1/4" high x 3 1/2" diameter, $30-35; cordial, 4 3/4" high x 1 3/4" diameter, $50-60. Front row, from left: 13 oz. footed tumbler, 7" high x 4" diameter, $35-40; 9 oz. footed tumbler, 6 1/4" high x 3 1/2" diameter, $30-35, 5 oz. footed tumbler, 5" high x 3" diameter, $25-30. All circa 1930s.

#7690 Monroe cut stem goblet, champagne, & cocktail with bowl in Asure Blue (Crystal stem and foot). #746 Sonoma Etch. Goblet: 7   1/2" high, 3 1/2" in diameter, $75-85; Champagne: 5 1/2" high, 3 1/4" in diameter, $65-75; Cocktail: 5" high, 3" in diameter, $55-65. Circa 1930s.

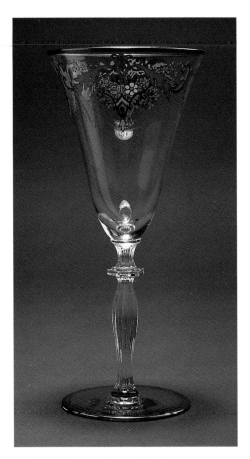

#7690 Monroe 9 oz. goblet. Enamel decoration. Gold band on foot. 8 1/4" high x 3 2/4" in diameter. Circa 1932. $90-100.

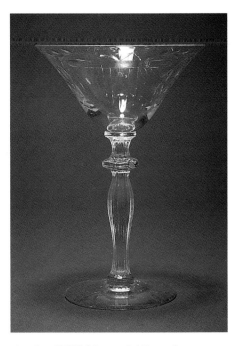

Another #7690 Monroe 5 1/2 oz. champagne. Crystal with unknown cutting. Circa 1930s. 6 1/2" high x 4" in diameter. $30-35.

#7690 Monroe 5 1/2 oz. champagne. Crystal with unknown cutting. Circa 1930s. 6 1/2" high x 4" in diameter. $30-35.

#7690 Monroe ice tea, crimped into vase in Spanish Red with Crystal stem and foot. 6 1/2" high. Circa 1930s. $75-85.

#7690 Monroe cordial. Cut Crystal. Circa 1932. 4 1/2" high x 1 1/2" in diameter. $45-50.

#7690 1/2 Duquesne Spanish Red 9 oz. goblet with Crystal stem and foot. Rim decorated with ornate Silver overlay. 8" high, 3 1/4" in diameter. $125-150.

#7695 Trumpet 11 oz. goblet with #734 American Beauty etch. Circa 1933. 7 1/2" high x 4" in diameter. $60-70.

#7693 Warwick cordial in Stiegel Green with Crystal stem and foot. 4" high x 1 1/2" diameter. Circa 1930s. $65-75.

Left: #7692 Churchill 11 oz. goblet. Spanish Red bowl, Crystal stem and foot. 8" high, 2 3/4" in diameter. $65-75.

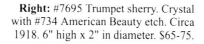

Right: #7695 Trumpet sherry. Crystal with #734 American Beauty etch. Circa 1918. 6" high x 2" in diameter. $65-75.

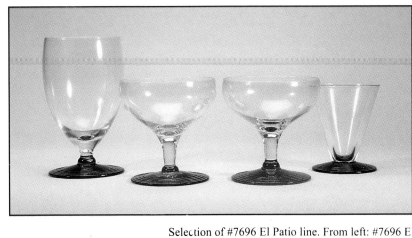

Selection of #7696 El Patio line. From left: #7696 El Patio 10 oz. luncheon goblet, Crystal with Stiegel Green foot, 5" high x 2 3/4" diameter; #7696 El Patio sherbet, Crystal with Amber foot, 3 1/2" high x 3 1/4" diameter; same sherbet with Tangerine (opaque) foot; #9075 El Patio cocktail, Crystal with Ritz Blue foot, 3" high x 2 1/2" diameter. Circa 1930s. $25-30 each.

#7700 Salem 1 oz. cordial. Crystal bowl, Ebony cased filament stem. 3 1/2" high x 1 3/8" in diameter. Circa 1931. $65-75.

#7705 Hopkins sherry with unknown etch. Crystal with Gold encrusted stem. Circa 1935. 6" high x 2 1/2" in diameter. $85-95.

Selection of #7711 Callahan stemware with assorted etchs. Back row, from left: goblet, 7 1/2" high x 3 1/2" diameter, $30-35; champagne, 5 3/4" high x 4 1/4" diameter, $25-30; wine, 6" high x 3" diameter, $25-30; ice tea, 5 1/2" high x 4" diameter, $25-30. Front row, from left: cocktail, 5 1/2" high x 3 1/4" diameter, $20-25; juice, 4 1/4" high x 3 1/4" diameter, $20-25; cordial, 4 1/2" high x 2" diameter, $30-35. All circa 1950s.

#7701 Fischer 10 oz. goblet. Crystal with Stiegel Green cased filament stem. Circa 1939. 7" high x 2 3/4" in diameter. $50-55.

#7711 Callahan champagne and sherbet. #733 Virginia etch. Crystal. Champagne: 6" high x 4" in diameter. Crystal. Sherbet: 4 1/2" high x 4" in diameter. Circa 1920. $18-20 each.

#7810 Monaco 9 oz. Crystal water goblet. #730 Adam etch. 6" high x 3 1/4" in diameter. Circa 1918. $25-28.

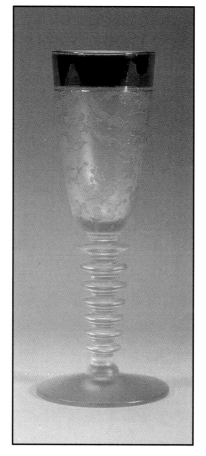

#7720 Palazzo cordial. Crystal. Sharon decoration. 4 1/4" high. Circa 1930s. $175-200.

#7720 Palazzo champagne. Crystal with Stiegel Green cased filament stem. Circa 1933. 5" high x 4 1/4" in diameter. $125-150.

#7813 Chapman 2 1/2 oz. wine, Crystal with Nanking Blue foot. Floral cutting. Circa 1922. 4 1/2" high x 2" in diameter. $25-28.

Sugars and Creamers

Two-Tone Danube sugar. Crystal with Nanking Blue. Circa 1920s. 4 1/4" high x 3" in diameter. $110-125.

#7857 Lando 12 oz. pilsner (ale). Crystal with #796 Floret etch. 8 1/2" high. Circa 1920s. $75-85.

Two-Tone Danube creamer. Crystal with Nanking Blue. Circa 1920s. 4 1/4" high x 3" in diameter. $110-125.

#8 Jered sugar and creamer. Stiegel Green with Crystal handles. Circa 1930s. Sugar: 3 1/2" high x 3 1/2" in diameter. Creamer: 4" high. $195-215.

#8 Jered cream and sugar in Old Bristol . Creamer: 4 1/4" high. Sugar: 3 1/4" x 3 1/2" high. Circa 1930s. $800-900.

#18 Barbara cream and sugar. Tow-tone Danube. Lydia cutting. Circa 1921. Creamer: 7" high; sugar: 6 1/4" high. $250-285.

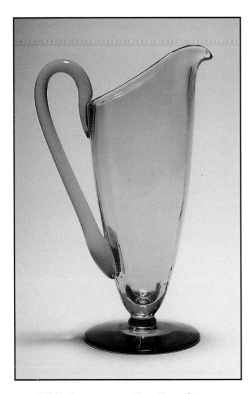

#18 Barbara creamer Two-Tone Genova. c. 1920s 6 3/4" high to lip. $110-125.

#43 LMX (El Mexicano) Mesa cream and sugar in Seaweed. Cream: 2 3/4" high. Sugar: 3" high x 3" diameter. Circa 1930s. $195-225 set.

#48 Benoit cream and sugar in Anna Rose with #758 Sunrise Medallion etch. Creamer: 4" high x 2 1/2" in diameter. Sugar: 2 1/2" high x 2 3/4" in diameter. Circa 1930s. $550-600.

#18 Barbara Crystal creamer with Shasta cutting. 7 1/4" high. Circa 1920s. $100-125 creamer only.

#308 Bangkok creamer in Azure Blue with Peacock optic. 4" high. Circa 1930s. $55-65.

#7621 Ringer sugar and creamer. Aquamarine. Circa 1930s. Sugar: 6" high (with lid) x 3 1/2" in diameter. Creamer: 4" high x 3 1/2" in diameter. $250-275 set.

Tumblers

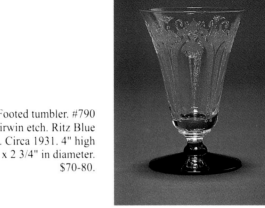

Footed tumbler. #790 Fairwin etch. Ritz Blue foot. Circa 1931. 4" high x 2 3/4" in diameter. $70-80.

#7640 Art Moderne creamers with Pillar optics. Left: Crystal with Ebony stem and handle. Right: Anna Rose bowl with Crystal handle, stem and foot. 5 1/2" high x 3" diameter. Circa 1930s. $300-325 creamer only, either color.

#7643 Golf Ball creamer and sugar in Ritz Blue with Crystal handle, stem and foot. Sugar: 4" high. Creamer: 5 1/4" high x 3" diameter. Circa 1930s. $300-350.

#33 Rawsthorne tumbler with Palm optic in Golden Iris. #545 Pickford 54 oz. jug. Golden Iris with Palm optic. Tumbler: 5" high, 3 1/2" diameter. $25-30. Matching flat bottom Jug: 8 1/4" high to lip. Circa 1930s. $325-365.

#7023 Cog Base tumbler. Crystal bowl. Anna Rose foot. Circa 1931. 3 3/4" high x 2 1/4" in diameter. $35-40.

#7587 Hanover 6 oz. footed/handled tumbler. Two-Tone Danube; Lydia cutting. Circa 1921. 5" high x 2 1/2" in diameter. $65-75.

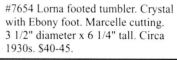

#7654 Lorna footed tumbler. Crystal with Ebony foot. Marcelle cutting. 3 1/2" diameter x 6 1/4" tall. Circa 1930s. $40-45.

Below: Back left: #7639 1/2 Ceredo footed tumbler with #781 fontinelle etch and Ebony foot. 4 1/4" high x 3 1/4" in diameter. $125-140
Back right: #7639 1/2 Ceredo footed tumbler with #781 fontinelle etch and Ebony foot. 3 1/2" high x 2 1/2" in diameter. $110-125.
Front: #7639 1/2 Ceredo footed tumbler with #781 fontinelle etch and India black foot. 3" high x 2" in diameter. $100-110.

#7654 Lorna footed tumbler. Crystal with a Stiegel Green foot and unknown cutting. Circa 1930s. 6 1/4" high x 3 1/4" in diameter. $22-25.

#7654 Lorna tumbler; Crystal with needle etch and Gold encrusted decoration. Circa 1920s. 5" high x 3" in diameter. $20-25.

7654 Lorna footed tumbler. Crystal bowl with ebony foot and Superba etch. 4 3/4" high x 3 1/4" diameter. Circa 1930s. $95-110.

#7703 Sextette Old Bristol 13 oz. tumbler. Ritz Blue bowl and foot with an Alabaster stem. 5 1/2" high, 3 1/2" in diameter. Circa 1930s. $140-160.

#7685 1/2 Ashcraft Stiegel Green 9 oz. footed tumbler with Crystal stem and foot. 6" high, 3 3/4" in diameter. Circa 1930s. $25-30.

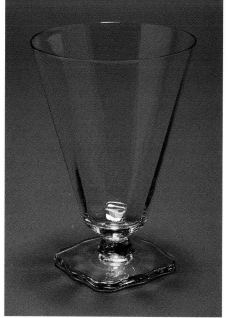

#S7659 1/2 Baldwin 13 oz. tumbler. 14K Topaz bowl, with Crystal square foot. Circa 1931. 5 1/2" high x 4 3/4" in diameter.

#8701 Garrett 9 oz. tumbler. Crystal. #730 Adam etch. Circa 1920. 5 1/2" high x 3" in diameter. $20-22.

#9043 Bowden 12 oz. angle-handled tumbler. Crystal Craquelle (crackled glass) with Amber handle and foot. Circa 1920s. 6" x 3 1/4" in diameter. $35-40.

#9074 Belton 11 oz. footed tumbler. Crystal bowl, Meadow Green foot. # 758 Sunrise Medallion etch. Circa 1931. 5 1/4" high x 3 1/2" in diameter. $75-85.

#9074 Belton tumblers. Left: Crystal with Venetian Green foot. Right: Two-Tone Arctic crackle Crystal with Venetian Green. Both measure 4 3/4" high x 3 1/2" in diameter. Circa 1920s. Left: $20-25; right: $25-30.

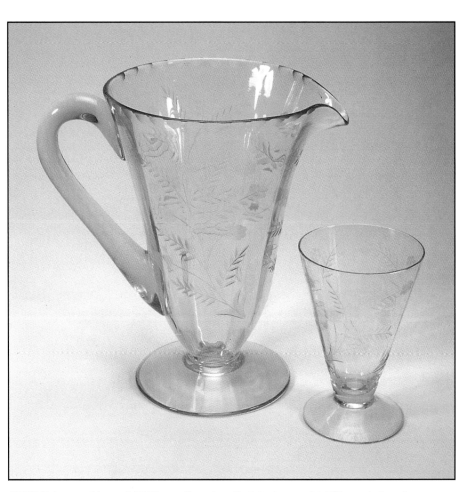

#9074 Belton tumbler and #37 Barry 40 oz. jug. Both in Azure with Pillar optic in unknown floral cutting. Tumbler: 5 1/4" high x 3 1/2" in diameter. Jug: 9" high x 6 1/4" in diameter. Circa 1930s. Belton tumbler: $40-45; jug: $350-400

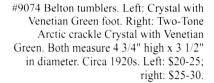

#9074 Belton Crystal tumbler with #785 Fernlee etch. Circa 1930s. 5" high x 3 3/4" in diameter. $40-45.

#9074 Belton tumbler with Golden Iris foot and enameled Rosamond decoration. 5 1/2" high x 3 1/2" diameter. Circa 1930s. $150-175.

#9074 Belton tumbler in Two-Tone Nubian. 4 3/4" high x 3 1/2" diameter. Circa 1920s. $125-150.

#9403—9 oz. tumbler with decoration #507. 3 3/4" high x 2 3/4" diameter. Circa pre-1920s. $50-55.

Left: #9416 Topeka 10 oz. flat bottom tumbler. Crystal with #743 Bramble Rose etch. Circa 1918. Straight top: 3 3/4" high x 2 1/2" in diameter. Flared top: 3 3/4" high x 2 3/4" in diameter. $20-22.
Right: #9715 Calhoun flat bottom tumbler. Crystal with #743 Bramble Rose etch. Circa 1918. $20-22.

#9417 Boyer tumbler. Crystal with #734 American Beauty etch. 2 1/4" high x 2" in diameter. $35-40.

#9715 Calhoun 2 1/2 oz. tumbler. Crystal with unknown needle etch. Circa 1918. 2 1/2" high x 2" in diameter. $15-18.

#9715 Calhoun 12 oz. lemonade tumbler. Crystal handled. #733 Virginia etch. Circa 1920. 5" high x 3" in diameter. $35-40.

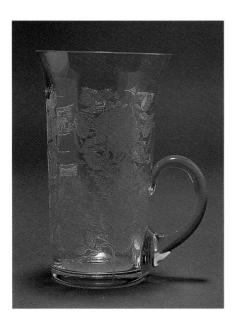

#9715 Calhoun 12 oz. handled tumbler. #734 American Beauty etch. All Crystal. Circa 1920s. 5" high x 3" in diameter. $60-70.

Vases

Included among the vases are the items the company called ivy and witch balls, rosebowls, and urns.

The artistry of Peter Gentile is evident in these two non-production vases are shown here with Italian bases. Gentile applied his distinctive Italian base to wares produced by the Fry factory, Morgantown factory, and his own Gentile glass factory.

Peter Gentile was one among many immigrants who enriched the American glass factories, bringing with them techniques and decorative styles from the European continent and using that knowledge to create innovative glasswares in America.

Gentile was born in Naples, Italy in 1884. Prior to leaving for America, he had apprenticed with several Italian glass factories for nearly fourteen years. Gentile's brother-in-law, Peter Picone, had emigrated and was working for the H.C. Fry Glass Company of Rochester, Pennsylvania and was able to convince Gentile and his family to join him at Fry (Wiley 1993, 32, 34).

Joseph Haden, Peter Gentile's former boss at Fry, lured Gentile to the Economy Tumbler Company in 1921. Steady work, six days a week, was just what the ambitious young artisan with a wife and family of five children was looking for (Wiley 1993, 34).

During his years with Economy, Gentile worked largely in the "jug" shop or the "head" shop. He had one of the highly skilled positions, he was a finisher. Gentile placed decorative handles on jugs and baskets and used precise shearing techniques to create distinctive shapes for some of the blown glassware of the period (Wiley 1993, 34).

Peter Gentile was also with the firm during the early Guild years, until 1947. Throughout the years, Gentile was restless and would often produce items after hours known as "end of the days," "trivias," or "whimsies." Also, the Morgantown Glassware Guild would allow employees access to the week's remaining melt on Thursday and Friday nights. Peter and his three sons availed themselves of this material to produce many wonderful, fanciful non-production items which are found and treasured today by collectors. These items included baskets, canes, horses, swords, and vases (Wiley 1993, 34-35).

#35 1/2 Naples marbled 12" vase with
Crystal Italian base. Not a production
piece, made by Peter Gentile, a
Morgantown glass worker, using a
Morgantown mold on his own time.
11 1/2" high, 5" in diameter shoulder.
Circa 1920s. $800-900.

12" vase made from #35 1/2 Naples mold with Anna Rose Italian base and Anna Rose applied rim. Non-production piece made by Morgantown glassworker Peter Gentile.Circa 1930s. $1000-1200.

Charlotte 8" vase in Randall Blue with Crystal Golf Ball stem and foot and Silver decoration. Circa 1930s. $200-225.

Right: #12 Viola 8" vase in Venetian Green with Gold decoration and Pin/Spiral optic. Circa 1920s. 8" high. $70-80.

#12 Viola vase, Crystal with #705 Pembrooke Poppy etch. 6" high x 6" diameter. Circa 1920s. $95-115.

#14 1/2 Jackson 8" vase, Stiegel Green with Crystal foot. $125-145.

#14 1/2 Jackson vase in Stiegel Green with Platinum decoration and Crystal foot. 6 1/2" high. Circa 1930s. $140-160.

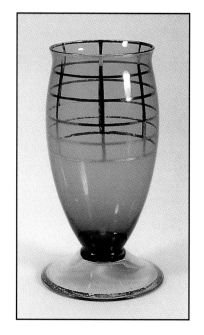

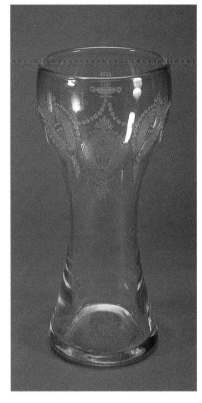

Below: #25 Olympic 12" vase. Crystal with Shasta cutting. Circa 1920. 12" high. $125-135.

#25 Olympic vase, Crystal with #730 Adam etch. 8" high. Circa 1920s. $225-250.

#16 Roby 10" vase. Crystal with flower design cutting. Circa 1918. 10" high. $95-110.

Below: #19 Frances 8" center vase. Crystal with unknown cutting. Circa 1920s. 4 1/4" high x 8" in diameter. $75-85.z

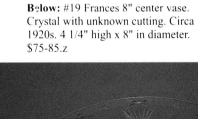

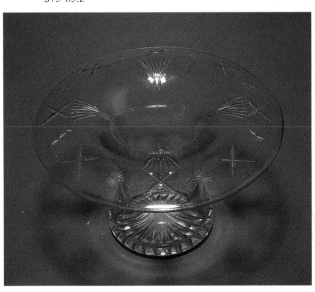

#25 Olympic vase in Alabaster with Gavotte decoration in Gold. 8" high. Circa 1930s. $300-350.

#32 Donna vase in Stiegel Green. 6" high. Circa 1930s. $65-75.

#35 1/2 Electra 10" vase with India Black handles and foot and Palm optic. Circa 1930s. $700-800.

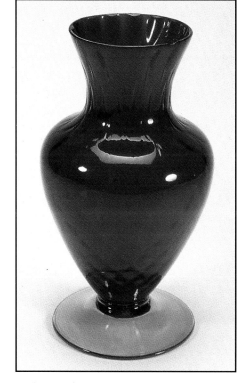

#35 Darwin vase, Ritz Blue with Peacock optic and Meadow Green base. 9 1/4" high. Circa 1930s. $350-400.

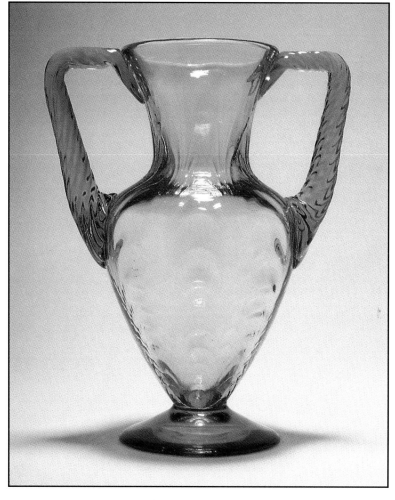

#35 1/2 Electra 10" vase. Anna Rose body with Meadow Green twist reed handle and foot and Palm optic. $650-750.

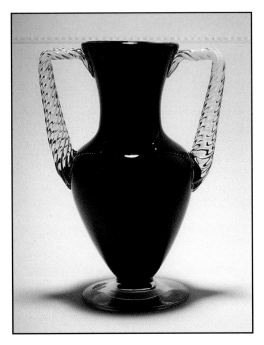

#35 1/2 Electra 10" handled vase. Ebony with Crystal handles and foot. Circa 1930s. $600-700.

#35 1/2 Electra vase. Meadow Green body, Palm optic, Jade green twist reed handles and foot. 9 1/2" high. $700-800.

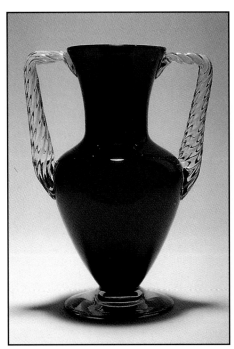

#35 1/2 Electra 10" vase in Spanish Red with Crystal twisted reed handle and Crystal foot. Circa 1930s. 10" high. $600-700.

#35 1/2 Naples 12" vase. Stiegel Green with Crystal Italian base. Circa 1930s. 12" high. $700-800.

#35 1/2 Naples 10" vase in Stiegel Green with Crystal Italian base and Silver decoration by Lotus. Circa 1930s. $750-850.

#45 Catherine 10" high vase. Jade with Meadow Green foot and crimped edge. Leda and the Swan decoration. Circa 1930s. $200-225.

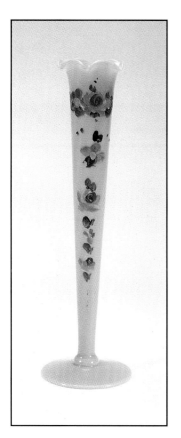

#45 Catherine 10" vase in Jade with a crimped edge and painted or enameled floral decoration. Circa 1930s. $175-200.

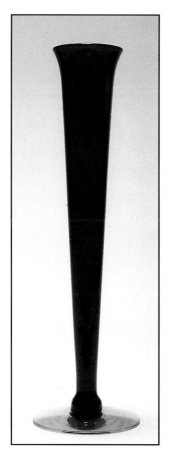

#45 Catherine 10" vase. Ritz Blue with a Crystal foot. Circa 1930s. 10" high. $100-115.

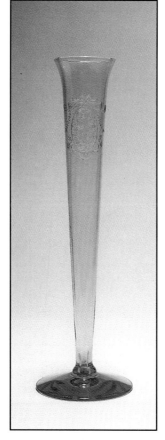

#45 Catherine vase. Venetian Green with a #758 Sunrise Medallion etch. Circa 1930s. 10 1/4" high, 2" in diameter. $200-225.

#46 Petite 6" vase in Venetian Green with Crystal foot and Palm optic. 6 1/2" high. Circa 1930s. $45-50.

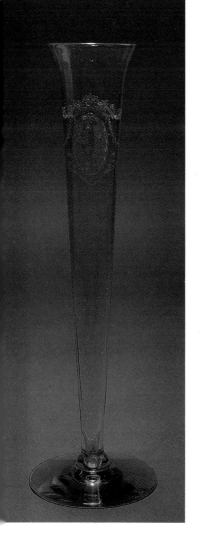

Left: #45 Catherine 10" vase. Meadow Green. #758 Sunrise Medallion etch. Circa 1931. 10" high. $200-225.

Right: #49 1/2 Juliet vase. Spanish Red bowl with Crystal foot. 8" high x 7" in diameter. Circa 1930s. $150-175.

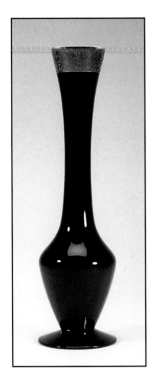

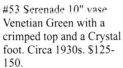

#53 Serenade 10" vase.
Venetian Green with a
crimped top and a Crystal
foot. Circa 1930s. $125-
150.

#53 Serenade 10" vase.
Ebony with Gold decoration
around rim. Circa 1930s.
$125-150.

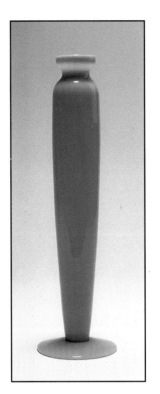

#54 Media 10" vase. Jade
Green. Circa 1930s. $125-
140.

#58 1/2 Engagement vase Jade green
body and foot with an Ebony ball. 9 1/2"
tall. Circa 1920s. $350-395.

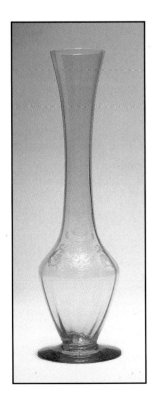

#53 Serenade 10" Meadow
Green vase, Straight optic,
#747 Biscayne etch. Circa
1930s. $160-175.

#53 Serenade vase. Yellow
Opaque. 10" high. Circa 1930s.
$150-175.

#59 Squat vase. Aquamarine with Palm optic. 6" high x 3 1/2"
diameter. Circa 1930s. $100-125.

Prior to leaving the Guild in 1947, Peter Gentile and his sons experimented with paperweights. Between four in the afternoon and twelve midnight, Gentile would often produce between ninety and one hundred paperweights. The plant managers would often pay for these items and would sell them. However, they were never sold as Morgantown products. The managers also provided Gentile with the addresses of customers whom he sold to directly (Wiley 1993, 35, 38).

In 1947, Peter Gentile left the Guild and opened his own business, the Gentile Glass Company of Star City, West Virginia (a suburb of Morgantown). He maintained a close working relationship with the Guild, however. Guild managers gave him some of their earlier molds. From these molds Peter Gentile's company produced many bowls, decanters, sugar and creamer sets, and witches' ball vases with his famous Italian foot.

Peter Gentile passed away at the age of 66 in 1951. However, the legacy of his craftsmanship and the company he established live on today (Wiley 1993, 38).

The El Mexicano "Snowball" vase would get a second life in the Guild years as part of the Crinkle line, sold with transparent colors (Wiley 1995, 2).

Ivy or witch ball in Ritz Blue with Crystal base. 6 1/4" high. Circa 1930s. $225-250.

#61 Ziegfeld 8" ivy/witch ball, Golden Iris, Crystal Italian base. Circa 1930s. $900-975.

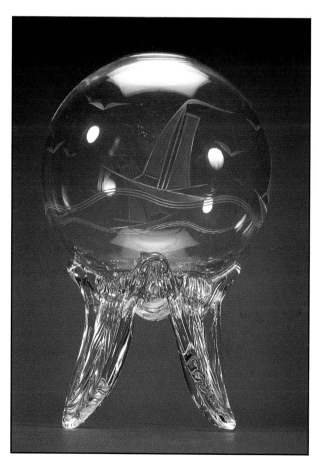

#61 Ziegfeld 8" diameter witch ball. Crystal with Italian base and unknown cutting. Circa 1930s. $900-975.

#61 Ziegfeld 8" diameter witch ball in Spanish Red with Crystal Italian base. Circa 1930s. $900-975.

#64 Neopolitan 6" diameter ivy/witch ball. 14K Topaz with a Spiral optic. Crystal Italian base. Circa 1930s. $700-800.

Two ivy/witch balls, showing variation in shape. Left: #64 Coventry in Spanish Red with Crystal foot. 7 1/2" high. Right: Ritz Blue with Crystal base. 6 1/4" high. Left: $200-225; right: $225-250.

#64 Neopolitan 6" ivy/witch ball in Jade with Crystal Italian base. Circa 1930s. $850-950.

#64 Neopolitan 6" ivy/witch ball, India Black with Crystal Italian base. Circa 1930s. $700-800.

#65 Roxanne 10" vase, Ritz Blue with scalloped edges and a Crystal base. Circa 1930s. 7 1/2" in diameter. $350-395.

#64 Neopolitan 6" ivy/witch ball with in Venetian Green with Peacock optic. Crystal Italian base. 22" high lamp. $750-850.

#67 Grecian 6" high vase. India Black with a Platinum #769 Sparta etch. $300-350.

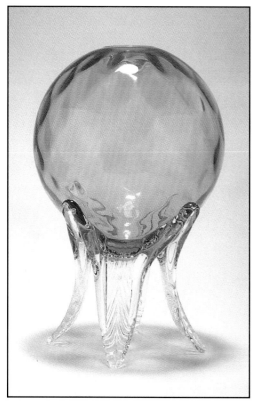

#64 Neopolitan 6" ivy/witch ball in Venetian Green with Peacock optic and Crystal Italian base. Circa 1930s. 9.5" high. $700-800.

#67 Grecian 6" vase in Stiegel
Green. Circa 1930s. $140-160.

#70 Saturn 6" Stiegel Green vase.
Circa 1930s. $200-250.

#68 Roma 10" vase. Ritz Blue
with a Crystal Italian foot. Circa
1930s. $700-800.

#71 Jupiter 6" vase, Jade Green.
Circa 1930s. $300-350.

#71 Jupiter 6" diameter vase in Stiegel
Green with Crystal Italian base. Circa
1930s. $750-850.

#73 Radio vase in Meadow Green with a Crystal base. 6 1/2" high. Circa 1930s. $250-300.

#79 Montagne 11" vase. Ritz Blue with a #7643 Crystal Golf Ball stem. Circa 1930s. 11" high, 4" in diameter. $395-425.

#76 Delores rosebowl in Stiegel Green. 5 1/2" high x 4 3/4" diameter. Circa 1930s. $140-160.

#73 Radio 6" vase, Stiegel Green with a Crystal foot. Circa 1930s. $250-300.

#76 Delores 6" rosebowl in Spanish Red . 4 1/2" in diameter at top. Circa 1930s. $140-160.

#87 El Greco 11" vase in Ritz Blue with Crystal twisted reed handles. Circa 1930s. $1200-1500.

#89 Toreador 15 1/4" Old
Amethyst vase with Crystal
twisted reed handles. Circa
1930s. $1200-1500.

#1933 LMX (El Mexicano) Snowball 7" flip vase in Pink Quartz. Circa 1930s. $225-250.

#90 Daisy 9 1/2" vase in Alabaster. Circa 1930s. $350-395.

Left: #91 Lalique vase. Crystal with matte finish. Ormalu metal frame (the frame was probably not done by Morgantown). 9 1/2" high. Circa 1930s. $650-750.

Right: #7601 Gardner 8" Flip vase. Azure Blue with a Palm optic. 8" high x 5 3/4" in diameter. Circa 1930s. $100-115.

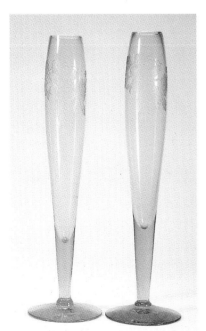

Left: #305 Luanna 10" vases with #811 Cathay etch in Meadow Green and Ginger. Circa 1920s. $150-175 each.

#7643 Charlotte Golf Ball vase. Crystal with Palm optic. 8" high x 3" diameter. Circa 1930s. $140-160.

#7643 Charlotte Golf Ball vase. Randall Blue with crimped rim. Circa 1930s. 8" high x 4" in diameter, crimp to crimp. $175-195.

#7643 Kennon 4" Ivy Ball in Alabaster with Gold painted nosegays. Circa 1930s. 6" high. $150-175.

#7643 Urn in Stiegel Green with a Crystal foot and Golf Ball connection. Circa 1930s. 6 1/2" high. $95-110.

#7682 Ramona line urn in Ritz Blue with Crystal stem and foot. 6" high x 3 3/4" diameter. Circa 1930s. $65-75.

#7681 Ramon footed cigarette urn and ash tray set in Stiegel Green. Circa 1930s. Urn: 2 3/4" high, 2 1/2" in diameter. Tray: 2 1/2" in diameter. $85-95 set.

#7643 Kimball Ivy ball. Ritz Blue with Crystal stem and foot. Circa 1930s. 7" high. $100-115.

#7688 1/2 Claridge 7" high brandy rosebowl in Spanish Red. Crystal facet stem and foot. Circa 1930s. $200-225.

The Guild Years, 1939-1971

Ash Trays

#130—9 3/4" diameter Ashtray in Gloria Blue; #129—5" diameter Ashtray in Gloria Blue. Circa 1960s. 9 3/4" ashtray: $25-35; 5" ashtray: $15-25.

Left: #9033 Lido vase, Crystal with #734 American Beauty etch. Circa 1920s. 8" high. $85-90.

Baubles

#1701 Double Baubles in Crystal. Circa 1970s. 23" high. $95-115.

#9033 Lido 6" vase in Spanish Red with crimped rim. Circa 1920s. $75-85.

Bowls

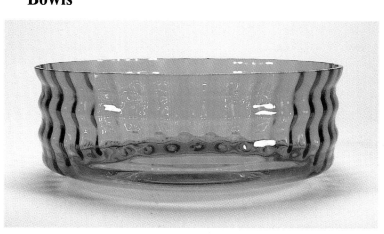

Peacock Blue bowl with optic, 8" diameter. Circa 1960s. $40-45.

#1102 Crown 9" bowl in Pineapple. Circa 1960s. $50-60.

#1962 Crinkle console (salad) bowl in blue. Circa 1960s. 4 1/4" high x 10" in diameter. $200-225.

Left and below:
#1962 Crinkle Icer with Insert. Green. Circa 1960s. Bowl: 4" high x 5 3/4" in diameter. Insert: 2 1/2" high x 3 1/2" in diameter. $45-50.

Boxes (Jars, Covered)

Bristol Blue powder box. 4" high x 4 3/4" diameter. Circa 1960s. $85-95.

#97 Dunstan 9 1/2" high stacked jar, Spiral optic in Evergreen with Crystal lid. Circa 1960s. $80-90.

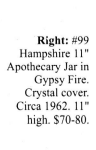

Right: #99 Hampshire 11" Apothecary Jar in Gypsy Fire. Crystal cover. Circa 1962. 11" high. $70-80.

#102 Ramsey 8 1/2" covered candy box. Crystal with Ebony cover. Circa 1960s. $45-50.

#1400 Diplomat covered jar in green. Circa 1958. 11 1/2" high x 4 1/2" in diameter. $60-70.

#1404 Doretta 6" candy box in Crystal with ebony lid. 6" high. Circa 1960s. $55-60.

#152 Juilette 8" Candy Box in Ruby with a Crystal cover. Circa 1960s. $40-50.

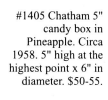

#1405 Chatham 5" candy box in Pineapple. Circa 1958. 5" high at the highest point x 6" in diameter. $50-55.

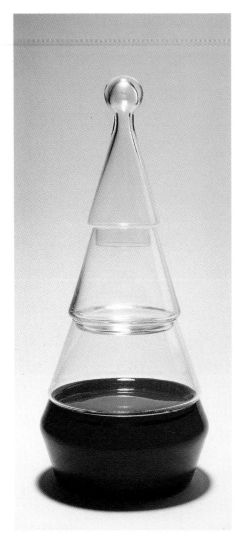

#9949 Christmas tree. 11" stack jar in Evergreen. Circa 1958. 11" high. $125-130.

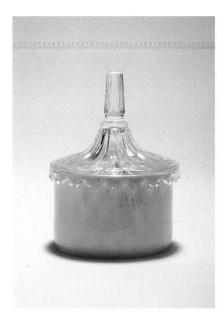

#9953 Flair 6" covered box in Peach (opaque soft pink). Crystal cover. Circa 1961. 6" high x 4" in diameter. $60-65.

#1410 Contemporary Tree. Four piece stack jar set. Top three parts Crystal; bottom in Ruby. Circa 1960s. 14 1/2" high. $125-150.

#1415 small Senator covered canister. White base with Ebony cover. Circa 1970s. 6 3/4" high with cover x 5" in diameter. $70-80.

Candlesticks, Candlelites, Flowerlites

#9953 Flair 8" covered box. Crystal with Peacock optic and Crystal lid. Circa 1960s. 8" high. $35-40.

#62 Chilton Hurricane Lite, crimped rim, in Burgundy. Circa 1964. 8" high x 4 3/4" in diameter. $50-60 pair.

(Without lid) #63 Lotus Flowerlite in Peacock Blue with Spiral Optic. 6" high, 5" diameter. (With lid) #63 Lorelei 8" Covered Box in Peacock Blue. 8" high with lid. Flowerlite: $25-35; covered box: $45-55.

#82 Cosmopolitan 7" slant candleholder in Gyspy Fire with matte finish. 7" high at highest point. Circa 1960s. $70-80 pair.

#88 Classic 4 3/4" candle-holder in Thistle. Circa 1960s. $40-50 pair.

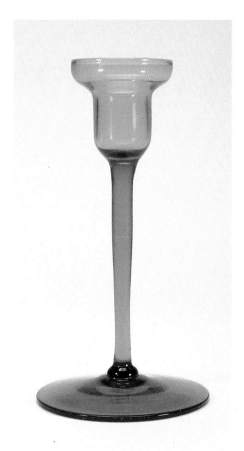

#81 Bravo 4 1/2" candleholder in Thistle. Circa 1960s. $45-60 pair.

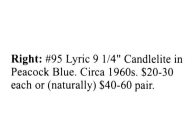

#80 Modern 6 1/2" candleholder in Peacock Blue. Circa 1960s. $35-40 pair.

Right: #95 Lyric 9 1/4" Candlelite in Peacock Blue. Circa 1960s. $20-30 each or (naturally) $40-60 pair.

#121 Tempo 5" Crystal candlestick
with a matte finish. Circa 1960s. 5"
high. $45-50 pair.

#1253 Cascade 6" candleholder in Pineapple.
Circa 1960s. $50-65 pair.

#1213/14 Winken and Blinken
4 1/2" candle light in Ebony and
White. Circa 1968. $60-70.

#1205 Spindle candleholder in
Ebony. Circa 1960s. 10 1/4" high.
$85-95 pair.

#1353 Art Nouveau 8" candlelite in Pineapple. Crimp
edge. Circa 1958. 8" high x 4 1/4" in diameter at top.
$50-60 pair.

Left: #2796 Coventry candleholder in Gypsy Fire with Crystal bottom. Circa 1967. 17" high x 3 1/2" in diameter. This product was marketed by Fostoria using a blown top made by the Morgantown Glassware Guild and a pressed Crystal base made by Fostoria. $140-160.

#2796 Coventry candleholder in Crystal with Moss Green base. Circa 1971. 8" high x 6" in diameter at base. This product was marketed by Fostoria. $90-110.

Above and right: #9921 Delphine Flowerlite with Crystal frog. Evergreen. Peacock optic. Circa 1958. 4 1/2" high x 3" in diameter. $35-40.

#9913 Federal patio light in Pineapple. 8 1/2" high x 4 1/2" diameter. Circa 1960s. $45-50 pair.

#9913 Federal Patio light in Ruby. 8 1/2" high x 4 1/4" in diameter. Circa 1960s. $50-60 pair.

#9930 Susquehanna candle vase in Lime. 5 1/2" high x 6" diameter. Circa 1960s. $20-30.

Back: #9928 Leeds flowerlite in Evergreen with Crystal frog insert. 4" high x 8" diameter, $25-35. Front left: #9920 Nova flowerlite in Steel Blue with Crystal frog insert. 3" high x 5" diameter, $20-30. Front right: #9920 Sharon flowerlite in Ruby with cystal frog insert. 3 1/4" high x 6" diameter, $20-30. Circa 1960s.

#9931 Florentine 5 1/2" candle vase in Thistle. 6" in diameter. Circa 1960s. $25-35.

Compotes

#12 Stella, 8", 6" & 4" compotes in Peacock Blue. Measure 5 1/4", 4 1/2", and 3" high. Circa 1960s. 8" compote: $15-22; 6" compote: $15-18; 4" compote: $12-15.

#12 Stella 8" compote in Burgundy, white spray. Circa 1960s. 5 1/2" high x 8" in diameter. The white inside was sprayed white by Beaumont Glass Company. $45-50.

#100 Kimberly 12 1/2" covered compote. Peacock Blue. Circa 1958. 12 1/2" high x 6" in diameter. $110-130.

Decanters

Left and above: #52 Tulsa 16" three piece decanter. Peacock blue. Circa 1958. 16" high. $85-95.

Egg Centrics

#1407 Egg Centric covered boxes. Ebony & Crystal, Crystal & Silver. Circa 1960s. Ebony & Crystal: $45-55; Crystal & Silver: $55-60.

#1962 Crinkle decanter in Blue. 8" high. Circa 1960s. $200-225.

#1408 Egg Centric
6 1/2" covered box.
Peacock blue. Circa
1958. 6 1/2" high.
$50-55.

Free-Forms

Free-Forms are well defined by Jim Wiley as, "... beautiful art ware creations and highly unusual glassware produced and marketed by the Morgantown Glassware Guild (Wiley 1996, 3)." In 1968, the Morgantown Glassware Guild commissioned Steve Britvec, the foreman for the Guild at that time and a glass blower since 1948, to create a series of artistic vases and platters called "Free-Forms." These were done as freehand work, without the use of any molds. Steve Britvec first encountered work of this sort being produced on a small scale in a Mexican factory in the early 1960s. Believing he could reproduce the technique on a larger scale, Britvec taught himself the art form (Wilcy 1996, 2).

Each Free-Form was individually created and, being freehand blown glass, no two pieces were exactly alike. The Guild marketed standard pieces, but every item was a little different. Free-Forms were used as hor d'oeuvre trays, fruit bowls, and conversation pieces when imagination failed. The Free-Forms all share a simple, graceful, fluid shape with upward sweeping ends (Wiley 1996, 2).

Steve Britvec states that he created no more than one thousand Free-Forms and that the Guild selected about sixty percent of these to market under the Morgantown name. Some of the selected pieces have the Morgantown name acid-etched on the base. Britvec also states that he made special presentation pieces as well (Wiley 1996, 2).

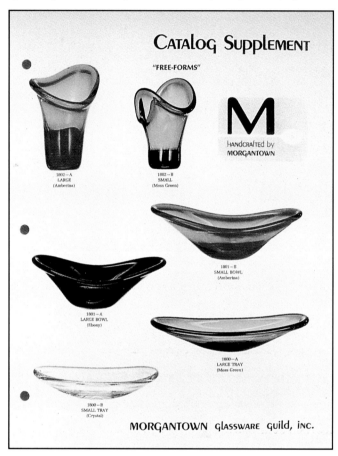

While using every color available at the Guild factory in the late 1960s, the most common colors for Britvec's Free-Forms include a Gypsy Fire and Ruby combination, Peacock Blue, Moss Green, and Crystal. Only a fortunate few have found Free-Forms with Ruby or Ritz Blue centers surrounded by a beautifully rolled crystal edge (Wiley 1996, 2).

Back: #1800 Free-Form line, in
Amberina, 13" long x 8 1/2" wide,
$80-90. Front: #1800 Free-Form line in
Midnight Blue with Crystal, 12 3/4"
high x 4 1/4" diameter, $55-65. Both
circa 1960s.

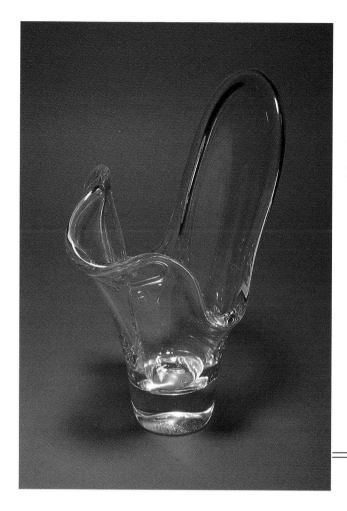

Left: Free-Form Crystal by Steve Britvec. Circa 1960s. 12" high at highest point. $80-90.

#1800 Free-Form line in Ebony. 1 5 1/4" high. Circa 1960s. $95-110.

Hang-One-On & Hang Ups

#3029 "Hang-ups" line. Back: snack bowl, 9 1/2" high x 5 3/4" diameter, $120-135. Front left: Bloody Mary, 6 1/2" high, $45-55. Front right: On-The-Rocks, 5 1/2" high x 2 1/2" diameter, $45-55. Circa 1960s.

#3038 Hang-One-On. Chains for men. Circa 1970. 7" high. $100-125.

Another version of #3038 Hang-One-On. Pearls for women. $100-125.

Martini Sets and Pitchers

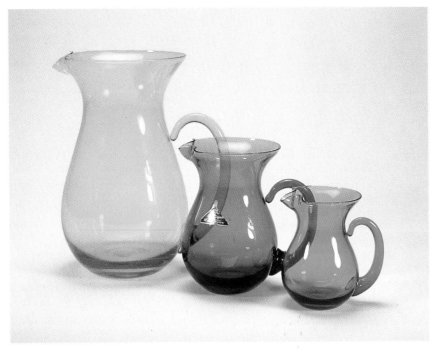

Selection of #78 Sexton martini mixers. From left: 46 oz. in Pineapple, 8" high, $55-65; 16 oz. in Evergreen, 5" high, $35-40; 6 oz. in Peacock Blue, 3 1/2" high, $35-40. Circa 1960s.

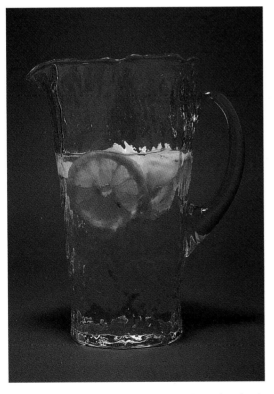

#1962 San Juan 54 oz. Crinkle Crystal tankard. Circa 1950s/60s. Crystal. 8 3/4" high. $50-60.

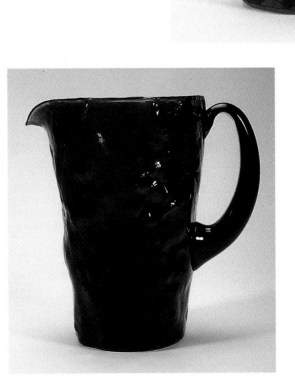

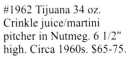

#1962 Crinkle martini mixer with chrome lid in Green. 9" high. Circa 1960s. $200-225.

#1962 Tijuana 34 oz. Crinkle juice/martini pitcher in Nutmeg. 6 1/2" high. Circa 1960s. $65-75.

#1962 Monterey 50+ oz. pitcher in Blue. Circa 1960s. 7 1/2" high. $140-155.

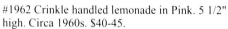

#1962 Crinkle handled lemonade in Pink. 5 1/2" high. Circa 1960s. $40-45.

#1962 Ockner Crinkle 50 oz pitcher. Burgundy. Circa 1958. 8" high x 5 1/4" in diameter. $95-115.

#1962 Monterey Crinkle 50+ oz. pitcher. Pink matte. Circa 1962. 7 1/4" high x 4 3/4" in diameter. $150-175.

#2007 Seville three-piece martini mixer set in Moss Green. Circa 1968. Pitcher: 9 1/2" high; Glass: 3 3/4" high x 2 3/4" in diameter. $45-50 set.

#9844 Swirl beverage set in Burgundy. Jug: 7 1/2" high; old-fashioned tumbler, 3 3/4" high. Circa 1950s. Jug: $85-95; tumbler: $15-20.

#9957 Wallace martini mixer. Steel blue. Circa 1960s. 7 1/2" high. $45-50.

#9895 1/2 Hoffman House three-piece martini set in Steel Blue with optic. Circa 1958. Pitcher: 9" high x 4 1/2" in diameter. Glass: 3" high x 3" in diameter. $50-55.

#9912 Accolade martini mixer in Topaz Mist. Circa 1960s. 10" high x 4 1/2" in diameter at top. $75-85.

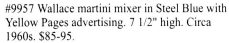

#9957 Wallace martini mixer in Steel Blue with Yellow Pages advertising. 7 1/2" high. Circa 1960s. $85-95.

Liquor Mixer

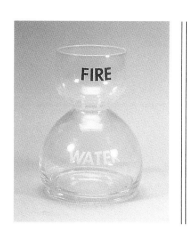

Fire & Water Liquor
Mixer, 3 3/4" high, 2" in
diameter opening. Circa
1960s. $20-30.

Moonscape Gifts

Moonscape vase, Peacock blue with Mist
base. (Fostoria design). Circa 1960s. $200-
225.

#3033 base of a Moonscape. 3 3/4" high.
Circa 1970s. $40-50.

#3033 Moonscape candy box with Mist
base and Steel Blue bowl. Circa 1970s.
$170-190.

#3034 hurricane candle in Moonscape.
Crystal bowl with Silver base. Circa 1969.
10" high. $140-160.

#3035 Moonscape 9 1/2" bowl. Crystal with
Silver base. Circa 1969. 6 3/4" high x 9 1/2"
in diameter. $125-150.

#3042 Moonscape covered candy in Steel with mist top. 5 1/2" high. Circa 1960s. $140-160.

Odd Balls

Mushroom Sets

#1413 High Mushroom 11" covered box made in white and ruby. Circa 1970. 11" high. $95-120.

Left: #1412 medium Mushroom covered box. Right: #1411 low Mushroom covered box. Both with Ebony base and Silver tops. Circa 1970. $95-120 each.

Above and right: #3010 Odd Ball Line. 8"
Bowl. All Crystal, cut by Mr. Lovejoy of
Duncan Miller Glass. Circa 1960. $125-150.

#3010 Odd Ball Line martini mixer in
Ebony with Crystal foot. Circa 1960s.
10 1/2" high. $90-100.

Left: #3010 Odd ball line 8" bowl
with enameled 8, Ebony with Crystal
foot. 8" high. #3010 8 1/2 oz. Old
Fashioned Odd ball with enameled 8,
Ebony with Crystal foot. 4 1/4" high.
Circa 1960s. 8" bowl: $125-150; old
fashioned: $55-65.

Private Molds

Three **Chanticleer** cocktails. Crystal
bowls with (from left), Shamrock Green
stem and Crystal foot, Amber stem and
foot, Gloria Blue stem and Crystal foot.
3 3/4" high x 3" diameter. Circa 1950s.
$60-70 each.

Left: Top Hat cocktail with Green bowl and foot and Crystal stem. Made for the Knickerbocker Hotel. Circa 1960s. 5 1/2" high x 3" in diameter. $60-70.

Three Top Hat cocktails, made for the Knickerbocker Hotel. From left: Spanish Red bowls with frosted stem and Crystal foot, $125-150; Crystal bowl with Amber stem and foot, $125-150; Ritz Blue bowl with Crystal stem and foot, $95-110. All 5" high x 3" diameter. Circa 1940s.

Old Crow 5 1/2 oz. cocktail. Crystal. Circa late 1960s. 6 1/2" high x 3" in diameter. $95-110.

Left: Mai Tai cocktail made for Trader Vic's restaurant chain. Crystal bowl with Amber **Polynesian** stem. Circa 1960s. 5 1/2" high x 3" in diameter. $50-55. Right: **Jockey** stem cocktail, 6 oz. in Crystal. Made for Gulfstream racetrack. Circa 1960s. 5 1/2" high x 3 1/2" in diameter. $45-50.

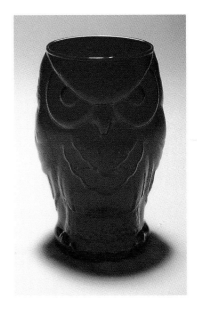

#1962 Owl 14 oz. Hiball in Ruby. Circa 1960s. 5 1/4" high x 2 3/4" in diameter. $75-100.

Russel Wright Designs

American Modern designed by Russel Wright, to accompany the American Modern ceramic line of Wright's made by Stubenville Pottery. No number. Came in five colors, Chartreuse, Granite, Gray, Coral and Seafoam. Back row: ice tea, $45-50; cocktail, $30-35; water, $45-50; juice, $20-25; cordial, $40-50; cocktail, $30-35; juice, $20-25; champagne or sherbet, $25-30; and the middle bottom is a dessert dish, $35-40.

The ice tea mesures 5" x 3" in diameter.

Stemwares

#3000 Festival Crystal footed ice tea. Circa 1960s. 6" high x 2 1/2" in diameter. $10-12.

From left: #3008 White Vision goblet in White, 7 1/4" high; #3008 White Vision wine in White with white on white decoration, floral border/band, 6" high; #3008 White Vision sherbet in White, 5 3/4" high. Circa 1970s. Goblet: $15-18; wine: $18-22; sherbet: $18-22.

Left: #3019 Pueblo footed tumbler in Ruby, 6" high x 3" diameter. Right: #3019 Pueblo sherbet in Ruby, 3 1/4" high x 3 1/4" diameter. Circa 1960s. Tumbler: $10-12; sherbet: $8-10.

#3047 Betsy Ross line: Left: goblet, 6 1/2" high. Right: wine, 5" high. Circa 1970s. $65-75 each.

Two "super-wines." Left: #3026 Tulip wine in Crystal, 12" high x 4" diameter. Right: #3025 Champagne flute in Crystal, 11" high x 5 1/4" diameter. Circa 1970. $65-75 each.

#6020—10 oz. Goblet in Peacock Blue and an Amber Juice. 5 1/2" x 3" in diameter. Goblet, 3 1/2" x 2 1/4" in diameter. Juice. Circa 1960s. Goblet: $6-8; juice: $4-6.

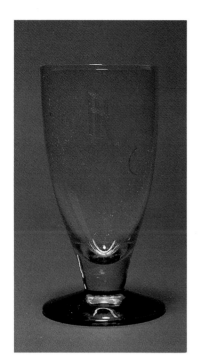

#7011 institutional ware Hartley goblet. Crystal bowl with Ruby foot and Illinois Railroad initials. Circa 1940s. 5 3/4" high x 2 1/2" in diameter. $35-40.

Assortment of institutional ware, all with Amber stem and foot. Circa 1940s. Back left: #7037 Harvard cocktail with optic. 5" high x 3" in diameter. Back right: #7039 Mariner champagne. 4 1/2" high x 3 3/4" in diameter. Front: Brandy. 4 1/2" high. $18-20 each.

#7701 Fischer cordial. Crystal bowl and foot with Spanish Red cased filament stem and Illinois Railroad cutting. 4" high x 1 1/8" diameter. Circa 1940s. $85-95.

#7039 Mariner whiskey sour, Crystal bowl and Stiegel Green stem and foot, Palm optic. 6" high. Circa 1940s. $30-35.

Left: #7180 Early American footed ice tea in Gloria Blue. 6 1/2" high x 3" diameter. Right: #7180 Early American 3 1/2 oz. wine in Gloria Blue, 4 1/2" high x 2" diameter. Circa 1960s. Ice tea: $12-15; wine: $8-10.

#7622 Majestic cocktails. Left: Smoke bowl and foot with Crystal stem. Right: Topaz Mist bowl and foot with Crystal stem. Both 6 1/4" high. Circa 1940s. $35-40 each.

Grouping of #7643 Golf Ball line in Harlequin pastel colors: Back row, from left: ice tea with unknown cutting in Peach, $40-45; goblet in Copen Blue, $40-45; parfait in Smoke, $50-60; 5 oz. champagne in iridized Yellow, $35-40; sherry in Shamrock Green, $35-40. Front row, from left: sherbet in Amethyst, $30-50; liqueur cocktail in Gloria Blue, $25-30; cordial in Topaz Mist, $40-45. All circa 1950s.

#8445 Plantation 9 oz. goblet. Spanish Red with Spanish red bowl, Crystal foot. Circa 1954. 7 1/2" high, 3 1/2" in diameter. $60-70.

#8446 Summer Cornucopia 7 oz. saucer champagne. Crystal. 1950s. 5 1/2" high x 4" in diameter. $150-165.

Selection of #8446 Summer Cornucopia. Circa 1950s. Back left: 7 oz. saucer champagne. 5 1/2" high x 4" in diameter. $150-165. Back right: 1 oz. cordial. 4" high. $225-250. Front: 4 oz. cocktail. 5" high x 3" in diameter. $125-150.

#7780 President's House line. From left: 11 oz. tulip champagne, 8" high x 2 3/4" diameter; 11 oz. water goblet, 7" high x 2 1/2" diameter; ice tea, 6" high x 2 3/4" diameter. Circa 1960s. $30-35 each.

Sugars and Creamers

Cream and sugar in Moss Green. Creamer: 4 1/2" high. Sugar: 2 1/2" high x 3 3/4" diameter. Circa 1960s. $35-40.

#9961 cream and sugar in Burgundy. Creamer: 3" high. Sugar: 3" high x 2 3/4" diameter. Circa 1960s. $40-45.

Tumblers

#1962 Ockner footed tumbler in Black. 5" high. #1962 Ockner 64 oz. jug. Black. 7" to lip. Circa 1960s. Tumbler: $45-50; jug: $175-195.

Selection of #1928 Ivy line in Stiegel Green, Emerald, Topaz, and Meadow or Light Green. (This is a combination of tumblers and stemwares.) Back row, from left: ice tea, juice tumbler, water goblet. Front row, from left: sherbet, wine, bowl. Circa 1950s. $45-50 each.

#2820 On-The-Rocks 10 oz. Crystal tumbler. Circa 1970. 4" high x 3 1/2" in diameter. $25-28.

Left: #1962 Crinkle water glasses. From left, Randall Blue, Gloria Blue, Peacock Blue. All 5" high, circa 1960s. $10-12 each.

☞

Left: #3000 Festival footed ice tea in Crystal. 6" high. Right: #3000 6oz. juice in Crystal. 3 3/4" high. Circa 1960s. Ice tea: $8-10; juice: $6-8.

#3055 19th Hole On-The-Rocks footed tumbler. White opaque bowl with green disc foot. Circa 1970. 4" high x 3 1/4" in diameter. $65-75.

#7780 President's House juice. Decorated with Seal of the President of the United States. 4" high. Circa 1960s. $35-40.

#9001 Billings tumbler with in Gloria Blue with a #808 Mikado etch. 5 1/4" high x 3 1/4" diameter. Circa 1960s. $15-18

#9872 Thumbprint 14 oz. ice teas in Peacock Blue and Crystal. 5 1/2" high, 3" in diameter. Circa 1960s. Peacock Blue ice tea: $8-10; Crystal ice tea: $6-8.

#9967 Challis line in Peacock Blue. From left: ice tea, 5 1/4" high; juice, 4" high; highball, 4 3/4" high. $10-12 each.

Left: #9968 Neptura double old-fashioned in Thistle, 3 1/2" high x 3 1/2" diameter. #9968 Neptura nappy in Thistle, 2 1/4" high x 5" diameter. Circa 1960s. Old fashioned: $10-12; nappy: $12-15.

Left: #9968 Neptura ice tea in Gypsy Fire, 5 1/4" high; Right: #9968 Neptura high ball in Moss Green, 4 3/4" high. Both circa 1960s. Ice tea: $20-25; high ball: $15-20.

Vases

Urns are included under this heading.

Selection of favor vases, all with Peacock optic. Back row, from left: Ruby, Evergreen. Front row, from left: Gypsy Fire, Burgundy, Steel Blue. 3" high. Circa 1960s. $45-50 each.

4" vase in Peacock Blue with Peacock optic. Circa 1960s. $50-60.

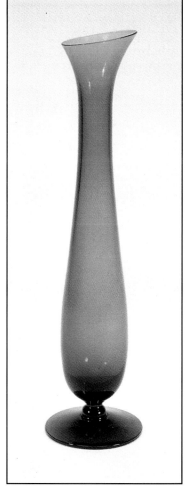

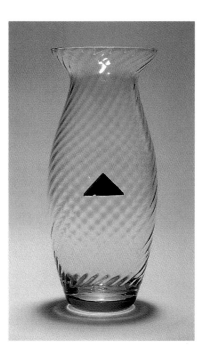

#18 Lynda 8" vase. Spiral optic in Thistle. Circa 1962. 8" high x 3 1/2" in diameter at top. $45-50.

#36 Lara vase in Burgundy. 10" high. Circa 1960s. $25-30.

#108 Wheatley vase in Peacock Blue. 11 1/2" tall, 3" opening. Circa 1960s. $45-55.

#114 Tuscany vase in Peacock Blue, 5 1/4" high x 4" high. Circa 1960s. $40-45.

#123-A Fairmont vase in Lime Green. 7" high. Circa 1960s. $35-40.

#113 Sovereign vase in Steel Blue. 10 1/4" high. Circa 1960s. $20-25.

#121 Charleston 5" vase in Ruby with Peacock optic. Circa 1960s. $40-45.

#123-A Fairmont vase in Peacock Blue. Circa late 1950s. 7 1/2" high. $30-35.

#1652 Norfolk 4 1/2" vase in Peacock Blue. 5" high. Circa 1960s. $18-25.

#9937 Revere vase in Ruby, 4 1/2" high, 6" in diameter. Circa 1960s. $25-35.

#201 Inverness vase in Peacock blue with Crystal foot and stem, matte finish. Circa 1950s. 9 3/4" high x 6" in diameter. $65-75.

#1962 Santiago vase in Amethyst. 4" high, 3 1/2" in diameter. opening. Circa 1960s. $35-45.

#1160 Baronet urn in Nutmeg. 6 1/2" high. Circa 1960s. $25-35.

#9942 Genoa vase in Peacock Blue. Circa 1964. 6" high. $50-60.

#1650 Seville 5 1/2" vase in Nutmeg. Circa 1960s. $15-20.

See #9969 Allegro vase in Peacock Blue on page 221.

Appendix I ❄

West Virginia Glass Companies, 1937

Name of Plant	Location	Principal Product	Name of Plant	Location	Principal Product
Adamston Flat Glass Co.	Clarksburg	Plate & Window Glass	Master Marble Co.	Clarksburg	Toy marbles & novelties
Akro Agate Co.	Clarksburg	Glass marbles	McBride Glass Co.	Salem (east plant)	Tableware
Alley Glass Co.	St. Marys	Marbles	McBride Glass Co.	Salem (west plant)	Lamps & chimneys
American Thermos Bottle Co.	Huntington	Glass Pistons	Mid-Atlantic Glass Co.	Lamberton	Stemware
Ball Brothers	Huntington	Fruit jars, glasses, etc.	Mississippi Glass Co.	Morgantown	Bent glass
Beaumont Co.	Morgantown	Tableware, hand made illuminating ware	Monongahela Valley Cut Glass Co.	Morgantown	Stemware & tableware
Bishoff Sons & Co.	Culloden	Lamp chimneys, novelties	Morgantown Glass Works	Morgantown	Tableware
Bishoff Sons & Co.	Hurricane	Illuminating ware	New Martinsville Glass Co.	New Martinsville	Lamp chimneys
Blenko Glass Co.	Milton	Colored sheet glass, off hand glassware	Owens-Illinois Glass Co.	Huntington	Glass containers
			Owens-Illinois Glass Co.	Owens	Glass containers
Borchart Glass Co.	Weston	Cut & etched glassware	Owens-Illinois Glass Co.	Fairmont	Glass containers
			Paden City Glass Co.	Paden City	Crystal & colored pressed glass
Bridgeport Lamp Chimney Co.	Bridgeport	Lamps & chimneys	Paramount Glass Co.	St. Marys	Stemware & glassware
Cameron Glass Co.	Cameron	Lamp chimneys, lantern & gas globes	Pederson Glass Co.	Lumberport	Flat glass
			Perfection Glass Co.	Star City	Illuminating glassware
Central Glass Works	Wheeling	Table glassware	Pittsburgh Plate Glass Co.	Clarksburg	Plate & window glass
Commercial Glass Co.	Fairmont	Opal glassware	Pressed Prism Glass Co.	Sabraton	Pressed glass
Crescent Glass Co.	Wellsburg	Novelty glassware	Quality Glass Co.	Vanvoorhis	Illuminating glassware
Dunbar Flint Glass Co.	Dunbar	Table glassware			
Eagle Convex Glass Co.	Clarksburg	Bent & convex glass & mirrors	Ravenswood Novelty Co.	Ravenswood	Marbles
			Rolland Glass Co.	Clarksburg	Plate & window glass
Earl, Shelby Glass Co.	Huntington	Communion glasses	St. Albans Glass Co.	St. Albans	Lamp chimneys
Erskine Glass & Mfg. Co.	Wellsburg	Illuminating glassware	Scohy Glass Co.	Sistersville	Window glass
			Scott Depot Glass Co.	Scott Depot	Lamp chimneys, lantern globes, etc.
Fenton Art Glass Co.	Williamstown	Colored Tableware	Sellaro and Martin	Star City	Lamp chimneys
Fostoria Glass Company	Moundsville	Hotel and dinner ware	Seneca Glass Co.	Morgantown	Hand blown tableware
Globe Glass Decorating Co.	Wellsburg	Decorated glassware	Sinclair Glass Co.	Ceredo	Automobile lenses, etc.
Hazel-Atlas Glass Co.	Clarksburg	Tableware, etc.	Universal Glass Co.	Parkersburg	Milk bottles
Hazel-Atlas Glass Co.	Grafton	Glass containers	Vitro-Agate Co.	Parkersburg	Glass marbles
Kerr, Alexander H.	Huntington	Fruit jars	West Fork Cut Glass Co.	Salem	Hand cut glassware
Lawrence Glass & Nov. Co.	Sistersville	Marbles & novelties	W. Va. Glass Specialty Co.	Wheeling	Tableware
			Wheeling Decorating Co.	Wheeling	Decorated china & glassware
Libby-Owens-Ford Co.	Charleston	Sheet glass	White and Bailey, Inc.	Clarksburg	Novelties & specialties
Libby-Owens-Ford Co.	Parkersburg	Vitrolite			
Louie Glass Co.	Weston	Tableware	Wissmath Glass Co.	Paden City	Colored sheet glass

Appendix II ❄

Skilled Labor and Wages at Morgantown, January 1, 1968
Vottero, Albert (compiler)

Punch Tumbler
blower $2.78
gatherer $2.56 1/2

Decor, Low Rate
blower $3.21
gatherer $2.94 1/2

Decor, High Rate
blower $3.24
gatherer $2.97 1/2

Paste Mold,
blower, $3.21
gatherer, $2.94 1/2
core gatherer, $2.52
handler 3.30

Iron Mold,
blower, $3.19
gatherer, $2.94 1/2
core gatherer, $2.57 1/2
handler $3.30

Drawn Stemware
blower, $2.93
gatherer, $2.69 1/2
finisherer $2.93

Drop Stemware
blower $3.10 1/2
gatherer $2.85
finishcr $3.10 1/2

Pressed Stemware
blower $2.93
finisher $3.03 1/2
gatherer $2.69 1/2
presser $2.75

Pressed Stemware Fostoria Method.
blower $2.88 1/2
finisher $3.03
gatherer $2.65 1/2
presser $2.88
stem gatherer $2.52 1/2.

Misc. Wages January 1, 1968
Hot Metal Department

Carry Over $2.16
Carry In $2.16
Hold Molds $2.16
Crack Off $2.19
Burn Off $2.19
Cut Down Hokey Pokey $2.22 1/2
Bit Gatherer $2.22 1/2
 3" or over $2.28 1/2
Handle Gatherer $2.33 1/2
Ball Boy $2.22 1/2
Flasher $2.22 1/2
Water Crackler $2.22 1/2
General Labor $2.16
Batch Mixer $2.34
Helper $2.24
Mold Paster $2.16

Color Ware Dept.
Spec. Selector $2.20
Selector $2.10
Cell Packer & order Assistant $2.10

Carton Room
Carton Maker $2.16

Finishing Dept.
Cut Off $2.10
Smoothing $2.10
Glazing $2.27
Put on Glazer $2.10
Selector $2.10
Cell packer $2.10
Helper (Male) $2.16

Lehr & Selection Dept.
Lehr Unloader $2.20
Helper $2.16
Selectors $2.20

Melting
Furnace Men Night $2.60 1/2
Furnace Men Day $2.55 1/2
Assistant Furnace Men $2.48
Pot Fillers $2.48

Shipping
Shippers Helper (no one permanently assigned)

Bibliography

Anonymous. *The Fire That Never Dies.* Morgantown, West Virginia: Morgantown Glassware Guild, Inc., n.d.

Britvec, Steve. "How Is Cased Glass Made?" *Topics. Old Morgantown Glass Collectors' Guild, Inc.* Vol. 3(4), Fall 1992. p. 2.

Bureau of Industrail Hygiene. *A Report on the Glass Industry in West Virginia.* West Virginia: State Health Department. (study conducted in winter of 1937-38.)

Callahan, James Morton. *History of the Making of Morgantown, West Virginia. A Type Study in Trans-Appalachian Local History.* Morgantown, West Virginia: West Virginia University Studies in History, 1926.

China, Glass and Lamps. "Morgantown Glass Works is New Name For Economy Factory at Morgantown. Name Used When Factory Was Started Over 30 Years Ago Again Resumed. History of Morgantown Factory Shows Steady and Healthy Growth With Product Constantly Improved." July 1, 1929, pp. 11-12.

_____. "New Wares For 1934 Featured Successful Exhibitions For Trade. Advance in Dinnerware Design and Decoration Received Wide Attention. Attendance and Business in Pittsburgh Well Ahead of 1933. Return of Liquors Helped Glassware." 1934, pp. 11-16.

Core, Earl L. *The Monongalia Story. A Bicentennial History.* Volumes I, IV, & V. Parsons, West Virginia: McClain Printing Company, 1982.

DuBois, Martha & Miller, Sue Ann. "Recorded Interview with Mr. Oscar DuBois. Morgantown, West Virginia, Thursday, May 6, 1965." Morgantown, West Virginia: West Virginia University, 1965.

Florence, Gene. *Elegant Glassware of the Depression Era.* Seventh Edition. Paducah, Kentucky: Collector Books, 1997.

Gallagher, Jerry. *A Handbook of Old Morgantown Glass. Volume I: A Guide to Identification and Shape.* Independently published. 1995.

_____. "Morgantown. Class Glass." Glass Collector's Digets Vol. 3(5), February/March 1990, pp. 39-42.

_____. "Morgantown. The Decor Years." *Glass Collector's Digest.* Vol. V(1), June/July 1991, pp. 42-51.

_____. "Morgantown Glassware Guild. The Co-op Years." Glass Collector's Digest. Vol. IV(1), June/July 1990, pp. 21-30.

_____. "Old Morgantown Glass. 1931: A good year for concept, design." *Panorama. The Dominion Post Sunday Magazine* (Morgantown, WV), Sunday, October 15, 1989, pp. 8-9.

Haden, Linda (ed.). *Morgantown Glass Collectors' Manual.* Morgantown, West Virginia: Old Morgantown Glass Collectors' Guild, n.d.

Leasure, Leora. "Stems of Desire!" *Topics. Old Morgantown Glass Collectors' Guild, Inc.* Vol 7(4). Fall 1996, pp. 4-5.

Morgantown Glass Works. *Old Morgantown Glass. Catalog of Glassware.* Copyright Morgantown, West Virginia: General Office and Factory, 1931.

Papert, Emma. *The Illustrated Guide to American Glass.* New York: Hawthorn Books, Inc., 1972.

Phillips, Phoebe (ed.). *The Encyclopedia of Glass.* New York: Crown Publishers, Inc., 1981.

Piña, Leslie. *Fostoria. Serving the American Table 1887-1986.* Atglen, Pennsylvania: Schiffer Publishing, Ltd., 1995.

_____. *Popular '50s and '60s Glass. Color Along the River.* Atglen, Pennsylvania: Schiffer Publishing, 1995.

Turnover Topics. "For the Buyer of First Quality Blown Glass, Pressed Glass, Dinnerware, Pottery." Number 7, March 1935.

United States Tariff Commission. *Household Glassware: Former Workers of the Morgantown Glassware Guild, Inc., Morgantown, West Virginia.* Washington, D.C.: TC Publication 456, 1972.

Vottero, Albert (compiler). *Illuminating and Tableware Rates. Compiled from Information Submitted to this Office by Hand Plant Companies.* Toledo, Ohio: American Flint Glass Workers' Union, March 1968.

Warrin, Edmondson. "And Now-A Toast! May Repeal Bring Fine Glassware Once More Into Its Own." *Crockery and Glass Journal.* October 1933. pp. 13-38.

Weatherman, Hazel Marie. *Colored Glassware of the Depression Era 2*. Ozark, MO: A Glassbooks Production, 1974.

Weiner, Robert Stanley. *The Location and Distribution of the Glass Industry of Ohio, Pennsylvania, and West Virginia*. Pittsburgh, Pennsylvania: University of Pittsburgh, 1949.

Wiley, James A. "Applied Rims." *Topics. Old Morgantown Glass Collectors' Guild, Inc.* Vol. 8(1). Winter 1997. pp. 2-3.

_____. "Free Forms." *Topics. Old Morgantown Glass Collectors' Guild, Inc.* Vol. 8(2), Spring 1996. pp. 2-3

_____. "Morgantown's Decanters." *Topics. Old Morgantown Glass Collectors' Guild, Inc.* Vol 7(4). Fall 1996. pp. 2-3.

_____. "Morgantown's Decorated Glass." *Topics. Old Morgantown Glass Collectors' Guild, Inc.* Vol. 7(3), Summer 1996.

_____. "Neat Stuff." *Topics. Old Morgantown Glass Collectors' Guild, Inc.* Vol. 8(2), Spring 1997, p. 2.

_____. "Peter Gentile. Portrait of an Artisan." *Glass Collector's Digest* Vol. 7(3), October/November 1993, pp. 32-38.

_____. Research notes.

Zembala, Dennis Michael. *Machines in the Glasshouse: The Transformation of Work in the Glass Industry, 1820-1915*. PhD. Dissertation for The George Washington University. September 30, 1984.

#9969 Allegro vase in Peacock Blue. Circa 1960s. 10" high. $50-60.

Index ✳

M

N

O

P

R

S

T

V

W